Joseph Levine

A Continuing Task

A CONTINUING TASK

The American Jewish
Joint Distribution Committee
1914–1964

Oscar Handlin

*Winthrop Professor of History
Harvard University*

Random House   New York

PREFACE

THIS BOOK APPEARS on the fiftieth anniversary of the founding of the American Jewish Joint Distribution Committee. In the half century since its inception this organization has devoted to humanitarian enterprises—in seventy-five different countries—over $800,000,000 raised chiefly through the voluntary efforts of the Jews of the United States. In the dark periods of the recent past its name was the symbol of hope for hundreds of thousands of victims of the cruelty of European society; it alone was in a position to save the lives of those doomed to destruction and to open a way of escape to the utterly helpless. Within the United States, on the other hand, the Joint Distribution Committee was the mechanism through which Jews could show their solidarity with those who still dwelt in bondage, and at the same time give practical expression to the ethical imperatives of their faith.

Yet no institution can simply be taken for granted by those who have inherited it. The participants in the work of the Joint—whether as beneficiaries or as donors—know what it does now. They also ought to understand how it came to be what it is. Its founders were members of a generation which has now passed away, and they lived in a world totally different from our own. The impulses which moved them are not altogether identical with those of the present, nor are the scale and methods of operation. There is nevertheless an underlying continuity of purpose that gives meaning to the experience of the organization through the years.

As the Joint moves into its second half century it encounters a world radically different from that of 1914. In the assessment of its continuing task, all those whose collaboration is essential to its success may find useful a historical survey of how it came to be what it is. Such an analysis will show what has changed and what has remained constant in its development, and will set in perspective the immediate problems of the present.

This book may also have a more general utility to those who are not part of the Joint's own constituency. Voluntary philanthropy has been a part of the American as well as the Jewish tradition. Whatever political differences may have divided the people of the United States from those of other parts of the world, Americans never isolated themselves when it came to their humanitarian obligations. All the citizens of our Republic have an interest in knowing how one group among them acquitted themselves of the grave responsibilities created by fifty years of tragedy and reconstruction.

CONTENTS

A Continuing Task

I

THE CHALLENGE

DURING THE HOT SUMMER months of 1914 an old society approached its death and a new one its maturity—both unwittingly. In the weeks that followed the assassination of the Austrian archduke, the lamps slowly went out across the continent of Europe—never to be rekindled in their previous form. On the other side of the Atlantic an ill-prepared people was as yet scarcely aware of the enormous global responsibilities about to be thrust upon them. The Great War and its aftermath permanently unsettled the lives of all men in the Western world, but none felt its effects more profoundly than the Jews of Europe and America.

Three great dynastic empires had dominated Central and Eastern Europe for almost a century. The Romanovs in

Russia, the Hohenzollerns in Germany and the Hapsburgs in Austria ruled great dominions that stretched eastward from the Rhine to the Urals and beyond. Their lesser neighbors—the kings of Rumania, Bulgaria, Serbia and Greece—survived only as satellites through the protection of one or another of the great powers.

Within these realms an unstable mass of some ten million Jews clung uneasily to their places in a society which made no room for them. Their traditional, ordered way of life, developed through centuries of adaptation, had been growing ever more precarious for fifty years; the events that began in 1914 would utterly destroy it.

In a broad band that reached from Danzig on the Baltic to Odessa on the Black Sea, in lands that had once been part of the Kingdom of Poland, lived the great majority of European Jews. In the twentieth century their position had become anomalous, for the special status they once occupied was no longer adaptable to the conditions of rapidly changing societies.

In earlier days the mass of the population had been entirely agricultural—peasants ruled and exploited by a minority of noble landholders. The Jews then had served a vital function; they were the intermediaries who handled the commercial and administrative functions of the economy and they supplied the skilled artisans who served the rural folk. The fact that in most places they could not take up farming was not then an insuperable handicap to a tolerable life. They could earn a livelihood in other ways.

There were sizable settlements in the larger Polish cities, but most East European Jews had been widely dispersed in tiny villages in close proximity to those of the peasants. In the *shtetl* the Jews had led an autonomous, self-contained existence, touching only infrequently the outer society of princes, peasants and priests. So long as they served their purpose, these communities were allowed to govern themselves and their members to go their own way in a style of life regulated by the precepts of a faith that ruled every aspect of daily existence by tradition. Set apart in appearance, clothing, language and habits, the majority and the minority inhabited distinct worlds that had little to do with each other.

Occasional outbreaks of violence showed how narrow were the limits of tolerance, and no Jew could ever escape the consciousness of his separateness and of his disabilities. But he had at least the solidarity of a cohesive community within which to take refuge. In Poland his Kehillah administered his own law, raised its own taxes and provided the agencies of self-help and education. Terrible though the years of hardship were in the seventeenth and eighteenth centuries, they only made the oppressed cling more closely together. Indeed, the Hasidic movement, which appeared during one of the harshest intervals of their experience, seemed to express the sense of unity and spiritual strength of these Jews.

However, the foundations of their communal order began to shake during the nineteenth century. Successive partitions had destroyed the loosely structured Kingdom of Poland and had distributed its territories and its Jews among more modern, centralized states. Prussia, Russia and Austria-Hungary were less inclined than the Poles had been to tolerate the distinctive status of an alien minority. Each step toward modernization and centralization weakened the old Jewish communities, for each demanded some degree of assimilation to the broader society as the price of citizenship.

In Germany and Austria relative toleration permitted the

Jews to retain their faith and gradually eased the burden of discrimination under which they labored. Indeed, by the end of the nineteenth century, even in the backward province of Galicia there had been some improvement in education and in the acquisition of artisan skills. In neighboring Serbia and Bulgaria the Jews also made a beginning toward modernizing their lives, protected as they were by the minority clauses of the Treaty of Berlin.

The autocratic czars, on the other hand, demanded full Russification of all their subjects and generally regarded conversion as a necessary step in the process. While inconsistency, inefficiency and corruption somewhat mitigated the harshness of the policy, Jews were prevented from moving out of the Pale of Settlement (the Polish and Ukrainian provinces) to the growing parts of the empire, and they were excluded from many desirable occupations as well as from the protection of their elementary civil rights. Rumania tended to follow the Russian pattern; despite the international guarantees for minorities at the Congress of Berlin, which established that kingdom in 1878, Jews were absolutely rightless aliens no matter how many generations they had lived where they were. In both countries peasant violence remained a constant threat, unrestrained and sometimes even stirred up by the government. And even in Germany and Austria, where there were no pogroms, rising popular nationalism contained a menacing element of anti-Semitism. The nineteenth-century conception of the state called for cultural homogeneity among its members, and whether beneficently in the form of emancipation or viciously in the form of persecution, it required the liquidation of the self-contained Jewish communities of the past.

Many Jews welcomed the prospects of leaving the ghetto and entering fully the life of the society about them, but relatively few wished to do so at the expense of their faith. In any case, it would have taken time and good will on both sides to lower barriers that had divided these societies for centuries. And time and good will were both lacking.

Moreover, sweeping economic changes throughout Europe compounded the difficulty of the transition. For a century after 1815, the Continent suffered from the pains of rapid growth. Its population mounted steadily; large-scale mechanized factories and farms replaced the small workshops of the artisans and the tiny holdings of the peasants; and great metropolitan cities drew together unprecedented masses.

In this fluid situation some Jews prospered as contractors, middlemen and manufacturers. But the overwhelming majority of those in Eastern Europe were trapped in a cruel predicament. Their numbers tripled between 1800 and 1850 and then doubled again by 1900, but no improvement in living conditions matched the growth of population. Indeed, in many places opportunities actually diminished. Large efficient units of agriculture displaced thousands of peasants, and also deprived the Jews who had served them of any function. The spread of factories took away the livelihood of the traditional artisans. Some, particularly in Russian Poland, left for the cities, where they became industrial laborers. But the majority, unwilling to take that drastic step, remained in the stagnant villages of the Ukraine, Galicia and Rumania, sunk in a suffocating poverty from which there seemed to be no escape. It was not untypical in such regions to find half the Jewish population scraping for its crust of bread in petty trade, while the rest—except for a few tailors and cobblers—were *luftmenschen*, people with no definite occupation who eked out a hand-to-mouth existence by their wits.

Decade by decade the situation became more precarious.

By the turn of the century half the artisans of Russian Poland were perennially unemployed. One representative statistic tells the story. In Odessa in 1900, 63 per cent of the dead Jews received paupers' funerals, and 32 per cent of the living received some charity.

Even the more prosperous were insecure. Merchants in Rumania and Poland, for instance, increasingly faced the competition of gentiles who did not scruple to use anti-Semitic boycotts to further their own ends. Jewish traders also suffered from the inability to secure loans from Polish credit institutions.

The shock of intellectual change was also unsettling. Exposure to the currents of Western ideas that swept across Europe in the nineteenth century weakened traditional assumptions and challenged the young to break with the communal past. Fresh opportunities generated a passion for secular learning frustrated by the restrictive policies of hostile governments which tolerated education only for a handful. But the curious could manage to read even the forbidden books, and the ambitious could break away from the villages for the expanded horizons of the cities.

In the 1840's, therefore, migration began to redistribute the Jewish population which, first in the hundreds and then in the thousands, escaped from the stifling hamlets. To begin with, the flow was internal, toward such nearby great cities as Warsaw and Lodz, or even—illegally—Moscow and St. Petersburg. But before long, others were making their way to Prague, Budapest, Berlin and Vienna. Here, beside the older traditional ones, new communities arose—secular in orientation, nurtured by an indigenous Yiddish culture, led by intellectuals and attractive to the working class. The socialist Bund enlisted the support of many, and a variety of Zionist groups gained adherents. Such people, more concerned with the future than with the past, were troubled by the abnormalities of the Jewish situation and sought to convert the masses from trade to productive callings. A few agricultural colonies were planted in the Ukraine, Lithuania and White Russia. There was a demand for vocational education that would prepare youth for the modern world more adequately than the *cheder* or the *yeshiva*. And in the first decade of the twentieth century, a cooperative credit movement took form that promised to further enterprise more efficiently than the familiar loan (*gemilath chesed*) societies of the past.

Eagerness to break away also turned the thoughts of some East European Jews to Palestine, where a few Zionist settlements took root. But that land was remote, still ruled by the Turks and peopled by backward Arabs. Therefore, for the most part, the Jews who decided to emigrate directed their steps to the West—to France, England and, beyond the ocean, to America. That stream began to flow in the 1870's and grew steadily in volume. Poverty and persecution pushed these people onward, and the czarist officials were perfectly willing to see them leave. Between 1870 and 1914 more than two million Jews entered the United States, fully 150,000 of them in 1906 alone. Here was their land of promise; here would develop a community that could come to the rescue of the Old World in its hour of need.

Americans were still hospitable to newcomers in the last quarter of the nineteenth century. The whole history of their country had been one of migration, and they took pride both in the diversity of their origins and in the place of refuge they had offered to the oppressed peoples of the world. Furthermore, the expanding mines and factories still called for additions to their labor force. Down to the outbreak of the war, the gates of the United States remained open to arrivals from Europe. Only the barest limitations of health and potential dependency excluded the least fortunate. Among those who then could still come were the Jews of Eastern Europe.

By 1870 those who landed in Castle Garden or other ports found already in existence a Jewish community formed by the migrations of the previous half century. The few thousand Jews of the Colonial period had laid the foundations; the structure was the product of the efforts of men who had settled in the United States since 1820. About 300,000 Jews had arrived there in the five decades after that date, mostly from Western Europe and particularly from Germany. They had entered an expanding economy, rich in opportunities; every region of the country felt the need for mercantile services that could be rendered by newcomers with experience in trade. As the years passed, the peddlers had accumulated the capital to set up shops, which in some cases had grown into establishments of impressive size. By the end of the century this had become a prosperous and stable group, which sustained its own synagogues, as well as cultural, fraternal and philanthropic organizations. Its leaders were men of wealth, especially the few influential bankers with connections to European houses; and its ideas, shaped by Reform Judaism, emphasized adaptation to modern life rather than traditional Orthodoxy, full participation in American society rather than separateness.

These people did much to ease the lot of the immigrants who came after 1870. Philanthropic sentiment and concern for the good repute of all Jews developed support for institutions to aid the adjustment of the newcomers and to sustain them when they became dependent. But a great gap developed between the older and the newer Jewish arrivals. The fugitives from the East European villages arrived in an America in process of industrialization. They found employment in factories and therefore clustered in the great cities, earning marginal wages and living under the depressed conditions of crowded slum quarters. There they formed a cultural order of their own, its language Yiddish, its media a host of *landsmannschaften* and other societies, a group of newspapers and the theater.

In America, as in Europe, the East European Jews tended to divide into two camps. The Orthodox labored to reconstruct in the strange cities as much as possible of the *shtetl* and of its traditional life. Their energies centered in the synagogue, in the religious school and in the difficult task of adhering in all strictness to traditional precepts. For them, the New World was above all the setting of an opportunity to practice without penalties the faith for which they had suffered in the Old.

For others, the migration was the occasion for casting off what they regarded as outmoded restraints. They had emerged from the ghetto into an open universe and wished to take advantage of their liberation. Since they were for the most part workers, their energies went into the labor movement, which grew steadily in strength after 1900, and their culture tended to be secular if not socialist in orientation.

Despite the divergence in ideology there remained important personal, social and cultural links between the two groups. Common ties to the districts of their birth, family connections, the Yiddish language and the problems of the slum quarters in which they dwelled created a basis for mutual understanding, if not always for cooperation or friendship. Both groups were products of the great migration that had transformed American Jewry by 1914 and both were remote from the earlier comers. Together, all these people constituted, if not the largest or the wealthiest aggregation of Jews in the world, at least the freest and most prosperous.

Although millions had departed from the depressed East European areas by 1914, the Jewish question there remained as grave as ever. An astronomical birth rate constantly replenished the numbers depleted by emigration, so that the situation continued to deteriorate. These poverty-stricken masses remained a challenge, troubling the consciences of their co-religionists everywhere. The occasional outbreaks of violence during these years were dramatic reminders that the problem was far from solved.

The middle-class Jews of London, Paris, Berlin or Vienna were themselves well adjusted. They considered themselves Englishmen, Frenchmen, Germans or Austrians, and they were aware that a great distance separated them from the miserable denizens of the *shtetl*. Yet, a powerful sense of obligation led those whose status was quite comfortable to respond to the needs of the less fortunate.

The traditional injunction that each individual must contribute to *zedakah*—that charity which literally means "justice"—remained strong. Felix M. Warburg recalled that during his youth in Germany "kindliness was the keynote of the household and from the first ten-pfennig piece that was received as an allowance it was made our duty to put one-tenth aside for charity, according to the old Jewish tradition." And aid was particularly due to other Jews, for the belief that all Israel was linked in brotherhood was nurtured by two thousand years of history. Centuries of experience had created a sense of mutuality; the group took care of its own, both out of the consciousness that no one else was likely to help and out of the reluctance to see its reputation suffer among other peoples. And then, among those who were themselves assimilating to new ways, there was a nostalgic respect for the stubborn guardians of the old tradition, who kept ancestral learning alive despite poverty and deprivation.

In Europe, assistance was largely the responsibility of the most prominent merchants and bankers who possessed the greatest resources. They acted as intermediaries at the sources of power to intercede for a mitigation of harsh conditions, and at moments of crisis they contributed to supplement the funds of local communities.

In the second half of the nineteenth century, crises became so general as to call forth permanent organizations. The Alliance Israélite Universelle, formed in Paris in 1860, aimed to work for the emancipation of Jews everywhere and to extend such relief as the depressed required. It was influential in the enactment of the minority clauses in the Treaty of Berlin and thereafter worked actively in Rumania; in Russia it aided emigrants, supported schools and provided relief during the all-too-frequent famines.

In practice this became largely a French association; Jews elsewhere therefore created their own national bodies. The Anglo-Jewish Association of London, established in 1871, operated in collaboration with the Board of Deputies of British Jews, which represented the congregations of England; it worked mostly in the Near East. The Israelitische Allianz zu Wien, set up two years later, took as the main setting of its efforts the nearby province of Galicia. And the Hilfsverein der deutschen Jüden in Berlin (1901) was mostly concerned with the problems of migrants in transit through Germany.

Until 1891 these organizations had depended for funds upon the benefactions of a few men of wealth. In that year Baron Maurice de Hirsch created the Jewish Colonization

Association (ICA), which he endowed with $10,000,000 and the assurance that the total would rise to $40,000,000 at his death. Convinced that there was no future for the Jews in Eastern Europe, he was determined to aid them to depart, hoping that most of them would find new homes as farmers in South America and also in the United States and Canada. To that end ICA sponsored programs for vocational and agricultural education. But since emigration would take a long time, ICA also understood that the Jews would have to become self-sustaining where they were. It therefore helped set up cooperative loan banks in Galicia, and granted subsidies to the Alliance and the Anglo-Jewish Association for work in the Balkan and Mediterranean areas. When Rumania excluded the Jew from the general schools, the Hirsch Fund set up special institutions to take their place. It hoped to direct migration constructively everywhere and to ease its hardships.

By 1914 the Jews of Europe had also founded a number of functional associations, to cooperate with the national ones. OSE (1912) directed its efforts at medical aid and the problems of sanitation. ORT, set up in 1880 by Baron Horace de Günzburg and reorganized in 1905 with ICA funds, sought to further training in handicrafts and in agriculture. And OPE (Jewish Educational Society) directed its efforts at modernizing Jewish education. All these groups aimed not only to provide relief in particular emergencies, but also to look ahead toward the process of extricating the victims from a hopeless future.

Until the outbreak of the war, the Jews of the United States played a relatively minor role in these activities. Their communities were too recently established and their local problems of immigrant adjustment were too grave to permit them to do much more. The Union of American Hebrew Congregations had included the reduction of discrimination among its objectives, and it attempted to assist newcomers. Also, from time to time the Independent Order B'nai B'rith sent aid through its European lodges. But there was no machinery for more systematic assistance; when pogroms or other disasters elicited her generosity, America contributed through one or another of the European organizations.

Yet there was a tradition of involvement with the affairs of Europe, not only among Jews but in the nation as a whole. The American government, by virtue of its special role in a democracy, felt some concern about oppression anywhere and was ready to express interest in the fate of all persecuted people. It protested, for instance, against the maltreatment of the Armenian minority in Turkey. By the same token, in 1902 it had complained to Rumania about violations of the rights guaranteed to Jews by the Berlin Treaty, and in 1911 it abrogated its commercial treaty with Russia as a sign of displeasure with czarist anti-Semitism.

There had also been a long history of voluntary benevolence in the United States to assist the unfortunate overseas. Americans had been generous in relief to the sufferers from European famine, and the wish to help had been a significant ingredient in the missionary activity that by 1914 extended around the world. In 1903 the Russian Massacre Fund, for instance, had appealed to all citizens of the United States for aid to the Jewish victims. It was to systematize such activities that the American National Red Cross had been created in 1881. Significantly, insistence from the United States persuaded the international organization to broaden the scope of its work to include the victims of peacetime as well as of wartime disasters.

All Americans collaborated in such endeavors, but in addition, individuals and groups with special ties overseas responded to a more intense urge for help. The Jews, who were themselves mostly immigrants or the children of immigrants, also felt this obligation. Even the poorest home had a *pushke*, or collection box, into which precious pennies went for the less fortunate, and every family sent remittances back to the old home—to the best of its ability. Rabbis such as Isaac M. Wise, Emil G. Hirsch and Kaufmann Kohler, who stressed the ethical element in Judaism, spread a sense of duty among the well-to-do members of Reform congregations. The growth of the problem of the East European Jews, and the magnitude of the response to it, early in the twentieth century led some men to consider the means by which to make this disorganized aid most effective.

In 1906 a small group of prominent leaders of German Jewish communal life in the United States met in New York to establish the American Jewish Committee. Wealth, power and single-minded certainty made Jacob H. Schiff the dominant figure in the new organization. He had come to the United States in 1865 from Frankfurt, a young man of eighteen, anxious to make his fortune. Twenty years later he was head of the banking house of Kuhn, Loeb and Company. Active in Equitable Life and the Union Pacific, Baltimore & Ohio and Pennsylvania railroads, his financial interests extended also to Mexico, Japan and China. Consciousness of his communal obligations led Schiff to philanthropy, and rejecting the laissez-faire philosophy of other moguls, he spoke up for the Negroes, for free public education, for the rights of unions and for the Child Labor Amendment. He also took an active interest in every phase of Jewish life.

Working closely with him were Louis Marshall and Cyrus Adler. The former had developed a successful law practice in Syracuse before coming to New York in the 1890's, where he earned a fortune in corporate work. He too was aware of his responsibilities and took an active part in the work of many organizations. Adler was the intellectual and scholar of the group, and the only one who was not a rich man. He was secretary of the Smithsonian Institution when he was asked to reorganize the Jewish Theological Seminary in 1901; his learning and sound common sense carried weight with the others.

Business, personal and family relations tied these people to the Warburgs, the Strauses and the Guggenheims in New York, to the Sulzbergers in Philadelphia and to similar families in other cities. Worried about anti-Semitism—the Dreyfus Case had not yet been settled and the embers of the Kishinev pogroms were not yet cool—they were profoundly disturbed by the threats to the gains Jews had made in the past century. The purpose of their committee was to protect the rights and ameliorate the condition of their co-religionists throughout the world. It thus fell within the traditions of both Jewish communal organization and American overseas philanthropy. But this was a loosely structured organization, which worked informally through the effects of a handful of men. Whatever aid they gave was through the European relief organizations and did not loom large in their consciousness.

Before long, however, the problem of relief for the East European Jews would override every concern. Since 1900 the plight of the impoverished millions had become ever more urgent. It required only the crisis of 1914 to reveal the desperation of the situation.

The implications for Jews everywhere were profound. In Russia and in Rumania it was evident government policy to force Jews to emigrate. Where would they go? As it was, Western Europe and the United States were over-

burdened; the densely crowded slums of Whitechapel and
the East Side were crammed to suffocation and seemed incapable of receiving the thousands who still clamored to
come. And entirely apart from the practical costs and
difficulties of accommodating the newcomers, another con-
sideration intruded upon the consciousness of the best-
intentioned West Europeans and Americans. Would not
the continued inundation by fugitives from the ghettos have
undesirable repercussions in the whole society?

Since the turn of the century, anti-Semitism had been
growing in strength, and now not merely among the crude
peasants of the backward countryside. In the salons of
Vienna, Berlin and Paris, racist doctrines were fashionable,
and some politicians in London and Washington were already receptive. Often the caricature of the East European
Jew supplied the material for their propaganda. If many
more were suddenly to leave their homes and pour westward, that would not only complicate the problems of adjustment but might also create a backlash of hostility that
could endanger the welfare of all.

Perhaps a refuge could be found in Latin America or
Africa where the fugitives could settle peaceably. Or perhaps their condition could gradually be improved where
they were. The first fourteen years were full of specula-
tions of this sort. But whether these people remained or
moved, relief was a constant and difficult problem.

This was the challenge as the catastrophe of war spread
across Central and Eastern Europe in August, 1914. The
implications would unfold steadily and tragically in the
next half century as crisis after crisis struck at the welfare
of European Jews.

II

THE FIRST

CATASTROPHE

1914-1918

As JULY, 1914, drew to a close, Europe blundered into disaster. Austria declared war on Serbia, and Russia then mobilized. Germany supported its ally and invaded Belgium. That brought England and France into the conflict. The world was ablaze.

After the failure of the initial German knockout blow aimed at Paris, the Western Front settled into a prolonged and bloody stalemate in the trenches. By contrast, the East was the scene of a war of movement in which a well-trained German army tested its might against poorly led and poorly equipped Russian manpower. While the Kaiser's troops were occupied in the West, the Czar was emboldened to send his forces on an ill-considered invasion of Prussia, only to meet disaster in the great battle at the Masurian

Lakes. Retaliation by the Germans brought them deeply into Poland, but not as yet far enough to seize Warsaw. After a brief lull in the winter of 1914–1915, the Germans resumed their advance; by September, 1916, they held all of Russian Poland and the Baltic provinces.

In this contest the Austrians offered their ally but meager assistance. In August, 1914, they had thrust quickly at the Czar's dominions; but the failure of their drive opened the way to a counterattack through Galicia and Bukovina. Thereafter the fortunes of war alternated between one side and another; and the massive armies moved back and forth across the tragic countryside. In the process they laid desolate the region with the heaviest concentration of Jewish population in Europe.

Everyone suffered in this modern war. Heavy artillery leveled the cities. The troops in advance and retreat and the refugees in flight leveled the crops and scorched the very earth. The normal lines of trade were severed. Order collapsed so that fires raged unchecked and pillagers were unrestrained.

The 9,000,000 Jews of Eastern Europe were particularly vulnerable. The general communal institutions offered them no protection and they themselves lacked the means of self-defense against acts of brutality by the invading or retreating soldiers. The men went off to fight and die, while the families remained helpless and dependent. There was simply no livelihood for the wives and children of petty traders and artisans, who lacked even the bits of land from which the peasant households could feed themselves.

Often, alas, the war opened an outlet for the hostility of the folk among whom the Jews lived. The ancient heritage of hatred in Poland and Rumania made the Jews convenient scapegoats upon whom their suffering countrymen could displace all aggression. The Russian government hoped to win over the majority and therefore did not discourage, and indeed sometimes openly egged on, the disorderly mobs to acts of violence against the minority. Misery that was already deep enough in 1914 deepened to an almost unimaginable degree in the years that followed.

Immense numbers took flight or were forced to move. When the Germans first entered Poland they acted the part of liberators and sought the support of the Jews. That aroused the already deep suspicions of the czarist government. Yiddish was considered an enemy tongue, and newspapers in that language were suspended. The field commanders sometimes seized hostages and often ordered the evacuation of the doubtful group into the interior of the empire under the pretext of protecting them from the dangers of the zone of combat. In the first year 100,000 crowded into Warsaw and 80,000 more into Lublin, Petrokov, Kielce and Radom. Between 600,000 and 700,000 Jews fled eastward from the Polish and Baltic provinces, and another 100,000 from Galicia and Bukovina. A smaller but still substantial number of refugees moved westward, some 500,000 into Austria and perhaps 100,000 into Germany.

The movement to the West was relatively orderly. Those who found their way to Vienna, Bohemia or Moravia received some assistance from the Austrian government and occasionally found employment. It was true that they were regarded as interlopers, often had to live in heatless barracks and suffered from shortages of food and clothing. But their situation shone in comparison with those expelled to the East.

The shuffling columns of bewildered civilians in flight were then still unfamiliar. Where were they going? For how long? No one knew. The preponderance of women, children and aged increased the difficulties of migration, as did the unfriendliness of the surrounding peoples. There was no adequate transport. The deportees were sometimes thrust into cattle and freight cars to be shipped to unknown destinations; sometimes the open road was the only avenue of escape. And those in flight could be sure that any scrap of property left behind would be stolen or destroyed. Some such unfortunates had to make several moves; and others could not survive even one, for typhus, typhoid, dysentery and cholera soon made an ugly appearance. How many died? No one troubled to preserve the mortality statistics.

Wherever they went, these people could hardly fend for themselves. Occasionally they tried pathetically to set up their workshops or find employment, but given the disturbed conditions of the times they were not likely to succeed; if they did, that often aroused the resentment of the indigenous populace. Some 30,000 of them lived without shelter in the woods through a Russian winter. When their pitiful resources gave out, starvation became commonplace. In 1917, 27,000 of the 38,000 Jews in Bialystok were starving; 350,000 in Warsaw depended on charity for their daily crust of bread.

Worst off were the residents of Galicia and Bukovina; the latter once relatively prosperous, the former always poor. By 1917 they suffered alike in fearful degradation. Six times the armies had marched across their soil and now only 500,000 remained of a Jewish population once more than twice as large. A newspaper correspondent in Lemberg penetrated in horror the "dens of naked, starving people—people driven insane by what they had experienced." The end of the fighting found the whole area desolate.

Rumania, which entered the conflict late and was quickly subdued, experienced only four months of actual combat;

yet it too suffered from the destruction of property and the disruption of trade. The war also created difficulties around the fringes of Eastern Europe. Parts of Serbia, Bulgaria and Greece were ravaged by long, savage campaigns; and the battles of Gallipoli and the Dardanelles drove thousands of Jewish refugees to Constantinople.

Turkey's entry as an ally of Germany and as a foe of Russia created a desperate situation for the Jewish communities in Palestine. The pioneer agricultural settlements immediately lost the market for their products in Western Europe. The rest of the population consisted in 1914 largely of clusters of aged pensioners, rabbis and scholars who had come to the Holy Land to study and who lived on remittances from abroad. A number of asylums and other institutions also depended on foreign support. The severance of relations with the Czar immediately impoverished these 60,000 Jews. Furthermore, the Russians among them were at once suspect as enemy aliens; and there was reason to fear that they might meet the same fate as the Armenians, who were already victims of persecution. Henry Morgenthau, Sr., then United States ambassador to the Turkish government, cabled on August 31, 1914, to Louis Marshall and Jacob Schiff for $50,000 for immediate aid.

Fully 85 per cent of the Jews were poor; they suffered from runaway inflation, from the lack of fuel in the winter and from the shortage of food always. Hunger, cholera and spotted fever raised the death rate from 27.6 per thousand among Sephardim in 1913–1914 to 96.3 in 1915–1916, and among Ashkenazim from 26.7 to 85. The number of orphans consequently increased. "Everywhere," an observer noted, "little Jewish children lay down and died in the streets; little families of two, three and four huddled together under the parental guidance of some ten-year-old older brother or sister. Most of them had not any shelter

for the night and they slept in some corner on the pave-
ment." The situation grew worse in 1917 with the American entry into the war and the threat of a British invasion
from Arabia. The Turkish secret police arrested some Jews
and expelled others; only the susceptibility of the officials
to baksheesh averted a total calamity until the situation eased
when Jerusalem finally fell to the British.

The less dramatic but nonetheless serious plight of other
groups of Jews made dependent by the war also called for
action—Russian refugees in Alexandria and students ma-
rooned in Switzerland, for example. These unfortunates
added to the roster of the needy. Help could reach them—
all the millions of them—only from America.

Local resources were totally inadequate. The self-contained *shtetl* was incapable even of sustaining the widows
and orphans or the disabled soldiers returned from the
front, and when it was dispersed its members were helpless.
Even the wealthy in the cities were hard pressed as trade
declined, so that the European relief organizations could
not themselves shoulder the burden. Only the ICA had substantial funds of its own and it could expend them only on
constructive, not relief, functions. The appeals for help grew
steadily louder as the war unfolded. In response, B'nai B'rith,
the Union of Orthodox Jewish Congregations, many *landsmannschaften* and countless individuals began to send remittances across the ocean.

The times were unpropitious, for 1914 was a year of depression in the United States. Under the circumstances,
these chaotic and disorganized efforts were hopelessly inadequate to the magnitude of the task, even in the early days
when it was possible to imagine that the war would come
to an early end. Yet, since American Jews were themselves

divided, it was not easy to devise a mechanism that would unite them all.

The American Jewish Committee had responded to Morgenthau's appeal by sending $50,000 to Constantinople through the good offices of the Standard Oil Company (of which the committee contributed $25,000; Jacob H. Schiff $12,500; and the Provisional Zionist Committee $12,500), and it allocated additional substantial sums for Europe later in 1914. But it realized that it was not representative of all American Jews and that it needed a broader framework for cooperation. The need became clearer in early October when the Orthodox Jews formed the Central Committee for the Relief of Jews Suffering Through the War. To prevent the dissipation of energies in separate and overlapping campaigns, the American Jewish Committee asked forty national organizations to meet on October 25, 1914. At that gathering Oscar S. Straus, Julian W. Mack, Louis D. Brandeis, Harry Fischel and Meyer London, who together commanded the confidence of every element, were charged to select one hundred distinguished individuals to act as the American Jewish Relief Committee, of which Louis Marshall was to be president and Felix M. Warburg treasurer. From this gathering came a plea for unity: "All Jews of every shade of thought, irrespective of the land of their birth, are solemnly admonished to contribute with the utmost generosity" to meet the superlative need.

With an initial grant of $100,000 from the American Jewish Committee, the Relief Committee set about the task of gathering funds as the year drew to a close. It worked up files of potential contributors throughout the country and designated state and local committees to solicit personally, by mail and through the press. But it was only slowly improvising a mode of operation. Meanwhile the Central Committee had expressed its willingness to cooperate but had retained its independence and conducted its own campaign through the synagogues and by the sale of special stamps. In mid-1915, therefore, the labor groups formed their own People's Relief Committee, under the chairmanship of Meyer London, making their appeal through the Yiddish press and unions. As a result there were three separate fund-raising organizations held together only by the fact that the Joint Distribution Committee of American Funds for the Relief of Jewish War Sufferers, formed on November 27, 1914, under the chairmanship of Felix M. Warburg, acted as a central disbursing agency. By December, 1915, these efforts had yielded some $1,500,000—not an impressive sum in view of the needs. There was widespread pessimism about the future prospect and a good deal of timidity about the immediate undertaking. As a result, some individuals and small societies continued to make their own collections for relief purposes.

It took considerable boldness, therefore, for Nathan Straus to demand that the campaign for 1916 set its sights at a $5,000,000 level, boldness that he backed with a personal gift of $100,000. To achieve that goal, the Relief Committee shifted tactics from personal to mass appeals, hoping to enlist in the effort not only the exceptional individuals but the larger numbers capable of adding to the total in smaller contributions. An opening meeting at Carnegie Hall on December 21, 1915, heard a stirring description of the plight of the war victims from Rabbi Judah L. Magnes, and collected $400,000 in cash and $1,500,000 more in pledges. Some weeks later, at the urging of the Senate, President Wilson was persuaded to proclaim January 27, 1916, Jewish War Sufferers Relief Day, and the Red Cross undertook to collect for the drive. National attention raised the amount gathered in 1916 to above $4,750,000.

That year Magnes went to German-occupied Poland. He

was then thirty-nine years old, a brilliant orator and a dynamic leader. Born in San Francisco and educated at the Hebrew Union College and the universities of Cincinnati and Berlin, he had held pulpits in Brooklyn and in New York and dreamed of uniting all the city's Jews in a great community under his leadership. Early an idealistic Zionist, he always bore a deep respect for the Jews of Eastern Europe who, he thought, incorporated a great spiritual heritage in their lives. Now he caught a glimpse of the wreckage of war and brought back a warning that $10,000,000 would have to be raised in the next year.

The 1917 campaign was more systematic than its predecessors. A meeting in Carnegie Hall, chaired by Schiff and addressed by Magnes and Mayor John P. Mitchell, raised $1,000,000. Another million from Julius Rosenwald was a further stimulus. Rosenwald, who had started life as a poor boy in Springfield, Illinois, and had made a fortune in the Sears, Roebuck enterprise, always insisted on the dynamic quality of his philanthropy. He made his gift conditional on the raising of the balance, and thus goaded the Joint agencies into a widespread canvass of the whole country. The Relief Committee was enlarged so that its membership represented not the national organizations but local communities, each of which was assigned a quota. Jacob Billikopf, then executive director of the Federation of Jewish Charities in Kansas City, came on to give the drive professional guidance.

In New York City, which was to raise $5,000,000, a list of 150,000 prospects was organized by occupations, and forty-seven volunteer teams, each under a captain, set to work to hit the target. A women's committee collaborated, newspapers and theaters were enlisted, and speakers, after the fashion of the liberty-loan orators, whipped up enthusiasm. A whirlwind ten-day effort brought the total over the top. More important, the experience developed methods later to be used with equal effectiveness.

American entry into the war momentarily raised a troublesome issue. The problems of European relief and prospective postwar reconstruction were no longer distinctive to Jews. It seemed to some at least, therefore, that their own efforts should be subsumed in a broader campaign that would enlist people of all religions and all national origins. A small-scale experiment in Wilmington, Delaware, seemed to indicate the value of the nonsectarian approach. A drive set to raise $75,000 in that city accumulated fully $148,000. The 1918 campaign, organized on that basis and using the methods already developed, collected $10,000,000 without difficulty and drew in contributions also from Canada, South America, South Africa and the West Indies. By then a powerful fund-raising mechanism had been shaped. Its full potentialities had only begun to be tested, but in these difficult war years it had made available to the Joint an income of $16,400,000.

The task of the Joint Distribution Committee at first seemed simple. It was to transmit the sums collected by the three American fund-raising groups to the appropriate agencies in Europe. A small subcommittee passed on reports from abroad and made recommendations to the Executive Committee of twenty-five, which voted allocations. The proceedings were informal, carried out by devoted volunteers. When unexpected difficulties occurred, the Joint was fortunate to have at its head a man able, powerful and wealthy enough to be able to cope with them.

Felix M. Warburg, the chairman, was the scion of an ancient banking house, born and reared in Hamburg. He had met and become engaged to Frieda, Jacob Schiff's only daughter; a year later he went to New York, where he married her and then joined his father-in-law's firm and became an American citizen. A fastidious patron of art and music and, like Schiff, a generous philanthropist, he found himself increasingly involved in the fate of those distant Jews to whom heritage tied him. To their welfare he would devote much of the next thirty years of his life.

To begin with, it seemed enough to transmit funds to existing European agencies in order to get the life-saving food, clothing and medical aid to those who needed them. The Allianz operated in the Austrian area through branches in Budapest, Lemberg and Cracow. The Hilfsverein was active in territories occupied by Germany, and its director, Swedish-born Bernhard Kahn, enlisted the aid of the military authorities. Russia at first lacked an equivalent. Then the Jewish Committee for the Relief of War Sufferers (EKOPO), originally a local St. Petersburg organization, expanded to encompass the whole empire.

Each of the national societies depended upon voluntary donations from its own members, and EKOPO, in addition, had the support of some government funds. But each also required and received help from the United States. The Americans were acquainted with some of the leaders of these groups—Max M. Warburg, the treasurer of the Hilfsverein, for instance, was a brother of Felix—and fiscal transfers could be made with relative ease. The difficulties created in 1915 by the need for routing aid to occupied Poland through a German committee aroused some suspicion in Orthodox and Zionist circles, but those abated when an investigation revealed the fairness and effectiveness of the operation.

The situation changed when the United States entered the war and severed all connections with the Central Powers. The Trading with the Enemy Act required special licenses for the dispatch of remittances, and the flow of information stopped. Shortly thereafter the revolution in Russia added to the difficulties by cutting off all connections with the outer world and terminating the work of EKOPO. At about the same time severe food shortages began to reflect the effects of the Allied blockade.

An ingenious makeshift device permitted the flow of assistance to resume after some interruption. In August, 1917, the Holland Branch under the direction of F.S. Van Nierop, of the Amsterdamsche Bank, began to act as intermediary, with the approval of the U.S. State Department. In the same month Boris D. Bogen and Max Senior, experienced social workers, left the United States to help organize the effort. Communication across the Atlantic was difficult, and the emissaries were often compelled to make their own policy and conduct their own diplomacy. But they succeeded in keeping open a neutral channel, through which some aid reached the distressed areas until the Armistice. Funds could go by way of the Dutch embassy in Berlin and consulate in Warsaw to the Polish Jews. Often, alas, there was nothing to buy with the proceeds. Although the two staff members of the JDC did their best to supervise, they could do little to regularize expenditures until the peace.

Elsewhere, the Joint used whatever means were available. The Chief Rabbi in Salonica, a local committee in Alexandria, an American who happened to be living in Switzerland, were pressed into service to help those about them.

Palestine presented the most difficult problem. It was necessary there to deal with unsympathetic Turkish officials, with two separate Jewish communities and with a host of marginal charitable institutions—some of them bogus; some, one-man enterprises.

Until the American entry into the war, aid dribbled to the Holy Land through a variety of channels. In the winter of 1914–1915, Maurice Wertheim had himself carried funds over. Some individuals, like Nathan Straus and Theresa Dreyfus, maintained soup kitchens on their own accounts or sent money directly to the needy groups with which they were familiar. In 1915, through the good offices of President Wilson and Secretary of the Navy Josephus Daniels, the Joint received space on the collier *Vulcan* in which to ship nine hundred tons of food and medicine. But most JDC funds were sent to the United States consulate in Jerusalem, which disbursed them through a local committee.

That mechanism collapsed when the consulate closed and direct communications between Palestine and New York ended. In June, S. Hoofien, the Dutch manager of the Anglo-Palestinian Bank in Jerusalem, agreed to act as the Joint's distributing agent, but for two months he received no instructions from anyone about how to proceed. Starting in August he began to receive substantial sums, but for a long time he got no written directions because the secret police intercepted his mail. He therefore had to improvise, borrowing heavily on his own responsibility in the faith that he would some day be reimbursed. He also had to outwit the hostile Syrian proconsul, Djemal Pasha. Hoofien might well have failed had he not managed to enlist the sympathy of Count Antonio de Ballobar, the Spanish consul, who gave him space, protection and information. Not until May 31, 1918, when the Zionist Relief Commission took over after the British occupation, was Hoofien able to unburden himself of his responsibility. Despite these impediments the Joint had been able to transmit to Palestine a total of $2,-257,300.

In all areas and through all media the Joint disbursed close to $15,000,000 during the war years. The national societies made the allotments through their connections with hundreds of local committees in the depressed zones. Most of the money went simply to keep people alive— for bread, coal, shoes and medicine. There were efforts also to protect the refugees; for a time EKOPO sent out fifty squads to defend the fugitives en route. Employment agencies were established to find work for the needy, and the existing loan societies were underwritten to help the productive. Within the narrow limits of an impossible situation, there was also an effort to sustain cultural institutions, to rescue the children and to lay a groundwork for reconstruction. Shoemaking and tailoring workshops not only supplied needed employment but also developed skills for the future. Trade schools, it was hoped, would do the same. The existing agencies for medical and educational assistance —OSE, OPE and ORT—were sustained in their work under trying conditions.

These fragmentary efforts revealed the larger implications of the Jewish problem. As soon as men looked beyond the emergency need for relief from hunger and destitution, they saw the grim future that still awaited the Jews of Europe. The war had only deepened the dilemma of a group which was not yet accorded a secure place in the whole society. When the Armistice came on November 11, 1918, Europe lay in ruins, and the Jewish situation was no better than it had been in 1914. Aid from the United States had mitigated some of the hardships, but the challenge from the past still remained. The only difference was that now an instrument had been created, in the Joint, that would be available for some measure of support in the years to come.

III

RECONSTRUCTION

1919-1924

ON SEPTEMBER 9, 1920, a meeting in Carnegie Hall mourned the death of two Americans in a war that for most of the audience had been over for almost two years. The photographs of the two men revealed them to be fighters of an unusual sort. Dr. Israel Friedlander, a bearded scholar in his mid-forties, held a doctorate of philosophy from the University of Strasbourg and was also a noted Orientalist; he had taught at the Jewish Theological Seminary since 1903. Rabbi Jacob Cantor, still in his twenties, smooth-shaven, was a recent graduate of the Hebrew Union College. Both were unlikely candidates for martyrdom. They had been shot by Red Army soldiers in the province of Podolia while attempting to deal with the unfinished business of the war. They had been on their way to seek out Marshal

Pilsudski in an effort to halt the pogroms that raged across the Ukraine.

In 1918 Eastern Europe lay in utter chaos. Four years of fighting had devastated the countryside and destroyed the cities. Normal life so long suspended did not readily resume its former course.

The Jews had been particularly vulnerable to the disaster; they would find it particularly difficult to re-establish themselves. Perhaps a million of them were homeless refugees, carried by the tides of conflict far away from the places of their birth, some of them to the remoteness of Siberia. Lacking news or information, they groped blindly back to where they imagined their friends and relatives might be. Weakened by hunger and by the lack of shelter, they imposed a disagreeable burden on every community through which they passed, left hostile feelings of guilt and resentment behind them. Everywhere thousands of orphans were unprovided for. Often, not only the parents but all close relatives had disappeared, leaving the children to roam in desperate gangs.

There was no interval of calm in which to begin the readjustment of these tragic victims, for the upheavals of peace were as upsetting as those of war. Revolution, political changes, nationalism and economic disorder left the region ravished in 1919 and 1920. Their deleterious effects remained even after the fighting had ended and the famine subsided.

In Russia the revolution of 1917 introduced a long period of uncertainty. The government had dissolved before the Bolsheviks assumed control, and the new rulers were slow to make their authority felt throughout the land. The Red and the White armies battled across the Ukraine in savage guerrilla warfare, and marauding bands swept through the villages, frequently just for the loot. Denikin's White army and Simon Petlyura's Ukrainian forces surpassed the Reds in savagery; but all singled out the Jews for depredation. In the resultant confusion, widespread pogroms offered an emotional outlet to the oppressed peasantry at the cost of fully 200,000 lives. In 1919, famine furnished the gruesome undertone to the tragic situation.

A mad war added to the misery. In May, 1920, the Poles, inflamed by nationalist delusions, marched into the Soviet Union. They penetrated deeply into the Ukraine before they were turned back, and then suffered in turn an invasion that brought the Bolsheviks almost to the gates of Warsaw. Hostilities ended in March, 1921, with no gains for either side, but with heavy Jewish losses.

Well into 1922, wandering refugees revealed the effects of war and hunger. A dispassionate observer found the situation in the Ukraine in April indescribable. "A mass of humanity of both sexes and of all ages—all in a fearful state as to clothing and lack of food" crowded the junction points. The floor of the Kharkov railroad station was "literally covered with people, old and young—men, women, children, infants—all starving and a number already dead." They could only escape "herded into boxcars, where they were packed as tight as they could be crowded in." To many the situation seemed utterly hopeless.

As the immediate hardships subsided, the deeper long-term problems became apparent. In Communist Russia the new regime began to transform the economy. The future order had no place for tradespeople; in a republic of workers and peasants, the landless, unskilled Jews were superfluous. Those who would not or could not move to the factory cities faced a blank future.

Shortly after the Armistice, pogroms in Lemberg and

Vilna had shown that Jews were not to have an easy time of it elsewhere in Eastern Europe either. Nationalism was the dynamic social force. The treaties of peace had broken up the great Austro-Hungarian and German empires and had erected in their place a chain of newly independent states between Russia and the West: Latvia, Lithuania, Estonia, Poland, Czechoslovakia, Hungary and Yugoslavia.

These governments were unstable. After a period of liberalism Hungary fell into the hands of Communist Béla Kun, and then was ruled by reactionary regimes. In Rumania, Poland and Hungary unscrupulous politicians sought to consolidate their power by popular nationalism, stirring up memories of past oppressions and hopes of future grandeur. All too often they expected to heal the social divisions within their countries by emotional appeals to unity. Since the maps drawn at the peace tables left pockets of minorities in each of these lands, it was tempting to make conformity with the majority an index of patriotism. These were ominous signs for the Jews, whose communities were still separate—if anything, more separate than before the cruel suffering of the war. It was, after all, hard for the victim of a pogrom to feel a great sense of identity with his assaulters. The formal guarantees of minority rights written into the treaties had little value under the circumstances.

Nationalism also deepened the dangerous economic consequences of independence. The new states chopped up the large economic units of the old empires, and Lithuania, Latvia, Rumania and Czechoslovakia were cut off from their natural markets in Russia, Poland and Austria-Hungary. In response, the unskilled rulers tried to develop autonomous commercial policies, with results that damaged all those who had formerly depended on trade for a livelihood. In practice, the desire to encourage national entrepreneurs was often directed at the Jew; the cooperative movement usually supported by the new governments also weakened his position, for he was frequently deliberately excluded from these organizations. Meanwhile he bore a disproportionate share of the heavy taxes. In Poland and Rumania, boycotts and quotas undermined the ability of the Jew to compete with his rivals, so that he suffered more than others from the effects of economic dislocation and currency depreciation.

Overt anti-Semitism was the product of these tensions even in Hungary, where it had not been common before the war. In Rumania, where such hatred had indeed been familiar, it grew more intense with the acquisition of Transylvania and Bukovina, which added to the number of Jews. Everywhere, the minority supplied a scapegoat for the frustrations of voters unaccustomed to the spirit or forms of democracy. By 1924 the prospect for a healthy adjustment in these areas was dim indeed.

The economic situation of the Jews had been unsound enough before 1914; the war had wiped out the wealthy and the middle classes and had compounded the misery of the masses. The plight of the hungry and the homeless shocked the consciences and sensibilities of all people of good will and particularly of those who had ties to the victims. Help was essential. How should it come?

Emigration no longer offered a means of escape. Nationalism had closed all the borders, and the poor lacked the means to take advantage of what loopholes existed. About 225,000 Jews had got out to the United States between 1921 and 1923. But then that country too had closed its gates with the laws of 1921 and 1924. This traditional safety valve for Europe's surplus population no longer functioned.

The Balfour Declaration had strengthened the Zionist

movement and had stimulated the hope that larger numbers of Jews would go to Palestine. But in 1924, although the gravity of Arab hostility was not yet understood, it was visionary to expect that the mandated area could receive a substantial portion of the 9,000,000 Jews in need. However many made their way there, the immense majority would remain in Europe and would need assistance there.

The older channels of aid were unavailable. Most local agencies had collapsed and the territorial changes of 1918 had disrupted the German, Austrian and Russian national organizations. Depression had depleted the resources of the remaining communal leaders, and sharp ideological differences divided the Zionists, the socialists, the Orthodox and the nationalists. Without help from America there was danger that all would drift aimlessly to destruction.

At first the situation was not well understood in the United States. The government and the Red Cross were prepared to relieve the distress of Europe on a nonsectarian basis, and the Congress set up the American Relief Administration—an unofficial, volunteer organization—with a grant of $100,000,000 to do so. There seemed no reason to give Jews preference. Herbert Hoover, who was to supervise the task of feeding the distressed, thus insisted in 1919 that all be treated alike. Felix Warburg succeeded in persuading him that that was unrealistic. The Jews were not, in fact, accorded the same rights or treated in the same way as the rest of the population. Historically and in terms of the existing situation they remained a separate community in a particularly dependent and vulnerable position. Unless that were recognized, they would be doomed to suffering. At the price of a special contribution of $3,300,000 by the

JDC to the general Relief Administration, the Jews were allowed to undertake their own errand of mercy to their co-religionists.

Fortunately, by then the JDC had both the will and the means to help. The successful wartime fund-raising campaigns had left a surplus of $1,500,000 at the beginning of 1919, and the mechanism of appeal remained intact. Meanwhile the dismal news from across the Atlantic stimulated the generosity of donors. In 1919 and 1920 contributions rose to $27,000,000.

Despite the magnitude of the needs, it proved more difficult to spend than to collect the money. The earlier intermediaries were no longer available; new means of administration had to be devised. The Joint ceased to be simply a disbursing medium; it had to administer its funds directly.

It assumed the task reluctantly. Its leaders had no wish to meddle in the affairs of Europe or to reform the lives of others. Wherever possible it worked through existing agencies, abjuring any political role, although to do so often resulted in a freezing of the status quo. Nor did it have a professional staff available; it was after all an organization devised for the immediate emergency of the war. The responsibility was there, however; no one else could bear it and for want of an alternative it fell to the Joint. But all involved agreed that the organization should offer what aid it could, make a start on reconstruction and then terminate its affairs.

Until it had the approval of the United States government the Joint worked through the field staff of the American Relief Administration, the United States Food Administration Grain Corporation, the Y.M.C.A., the Siberian Prisoners' Repatriation Fund, the Near Eastern Relief Commission, the Society of Friends, the Red Cross and the Polish Relief Committee. But this makeshift arrangement was by no means satisfactory. It could feed the starving but not make them self-sufficient.

In the interim the Joint began to hunt up a staff. In 1919 it became evident that its own representatives, even if temporary, would be useful in assuring prompt aid, in composing local factional differences, in cooperating with other agencies, in directing specialized activities and in reporting. Moreover, the presence of an American Jew had immense psychological value in reassuring his terror-stricken coreligionists that they were not altogether abandoned.

Personal qualifications at this stage were more useful than professional ones. A good part of the task was performed by volunteers. Dr. Julius Goldman, for instance, gave up a thriving law practice at the age of sixty-seven to go out as director in the field. He was to be succeeded by the banker James M. Becker, by the lawyers James N. Rosenberg and Howard S. Gans and by Judge Harry Fisher. Into the field there also went scholars and clergymen like Friedlander and Cantor, labor leaders like Max Pine, and idealistic young college graduates like Benjamin Pepper. Such men moved in and out of assignments as their hearts dictated and their schedules permitted.

Gradually, however, the elements of a permanent staff began to take form. Social work was then acquiring professional status and the Jewish agencies within the United States were preparing a group of experienced persons capable of taking an active role in the overseas effort. Boris Bogen, for instance, was a Moscow intellectual when he decided to come to the United States. He shifted from one job to another, yet had managed to earn a degree in education at New York University. After a period of service with the Baron de Hirsch Fund settlements in New Jersey he became superintendent of the United Jewish Charities in Cincinnati, and in 1913, field secretary of the National Conference of Jewish Charities. By then he was ready to assume overseas assignments. Increasingly the Joint would depend on such men to go into the field.

Through most of this period, the Soviet Union was a special case that diverged in experience from the other countries of Eastern Europe. The latter proved the easier to penetrate.

In January, 1919, the Joint sent Boris Bogen to make preliminary arrangements for the initiation of the immense task, and then two units of forty trained workers in American uniform, among them experts in sanitation, child care and economics. Although boundaries and jurisdictions were still uncertain, the agents struggled from regional centers to set up local committees to distribute relief, to rebuild homes and to revive decayed institutions. The *Westward Ho* had already brought the first cargo of food for free distribution in Poland; a merciful flow continued. To minimize the damage from currency depreciation, funds were sent across in dollars on a hand-to-mouth basis and converted as needed. In 1919 and 1920 the JDC spent well over $22,000,000 in this fashion. In addition it provided facilities for the transmittal of private remittances to Poland, handling well over $5,000,000 in the first nine months of 1920 alone.

Toward the end of 1920, with the peak of the crisis passed, it seemed time to end relief activities and to devote the remaining funds to reconstruction. Word of this decision brought consternation to Europe and compelled the extension of aid to the distressed beyond July 1, 1921, the date set for its termination. Nevertheless, emphasis in the next three years shifted from palliation toward rehabilitation.

At the end of 1920 the Joint had a balance of somewhat less than $6,000,000. From the field it got estimates that $14,000,000 more would be needed, and that it resolved to get by a national fund-raising campaign of its own. Once more the communities organized and thousands of volunteers canvassed the prospects. "Suppose *you* were starving?" That question, asked in 1921, had an all-too-vivid meaning for American Jews, who now knew the worst about events in Europe. Chicago alone that year received pledges of $2,000,000, New York of $4,000,000. While wealthy benefactors like Julius Rosenwald still took the lead, the number of small subscribers grew impressively—86,000 in New York alone. In the years from 1921 through 1924, the JDC collected well over $20,000,000.

This sum it had decided to expend in the "last period" of its work to restore the stability of Europe's Jews. A commission of experts under Lee K. Frankel traveled to Europe in the summer of 1922 and came back with a plan for doing so. The Joint in New York reorganized itself in five functional committees: on refugees (under David M. Bressler); on economic rehabilitation (under Herbert H. Lehman); on cultural and religious affairs (under Cyrus Adler); on orphans (under Solomon Lowenstein); and on medical and sanitary aid (under Bernard Flexner). Each established broad policies and exercised general supervision over its area of the work. The budget and departments in the field paralleled that structure. Local relief committees, gradually, were to become independent and self-sustaining. Each department was to get its task started, and then stimulate or create autonomous organizations to take over. The JDC would furnish the initial resources, but in the expectation that all would become self-sustaining.

The refugee problem gradually solved itself. Between 1921 and 1923, JDC efforts in Eastern Europe outside Russia helped 300,000 settle themselves. In the latter year the number of the homeless in Poland and Rumania had shrunk to 25,000, and the task of helping them could be shifted to the Emergency Refugee Committee formed with JDC aid. For better or worse, by 1924 Europe's Jews were reconciled to staying where they were. They had no alternative.

That made reconstruction all the more imperative. The familiar institutions of the small-loan *kassa* and the mutual-aid society were expected to help many to re-establish themselves. Although currency depreciation caused very great losses, it was "both inconceivable and indefensible" to "postpone the work" in disregard of the needs of the suffering masses. The effort to spread artisan skills also continued.

On May 3, 1924, JDC and ICA agreed to establish the American Joint Reconstruction Foundation, in which they would share control with representatives of European Jewry. The Joint contributed $3,000,000 and ICA $2,000,000 to its capital, to permit it to take over the tasks of rehabilitation in Eastern Europe—primarily through support of loan and producers' cooperatives, and through assistance to artisans. By 1924, 323 credit cooperatives with 115,000 members were in operation. With the aid of ORT a start was also made in vocational education.

The problems of health had received attention since 1921. In January of that year, a unit of eighteen physicians and other medical personnel arrived in Poland, to be stunned by the immense needs of a population in which tuberculosis, trachoma and favus were endemic. It financed and transformed some 500 institutions, including public baths, dispensaries, sanitaria, X-ray stations, and nurses training schools. A new health organization, TOZ, staffed largely by Polish Jews, picked up that portion of the Joint's work, although it still required financial aid from the United States.

The large number of orphans—60,000 outside Russia—also gave child care a high priority. Immediate aid and permanent institutions were both necessary. By the end of 1922, committees to deal with the problem had been created in each country, and in the next year the Joint was able to shift its burden in Poland to a Federation of Orphans' Care Societies (CENTOS). Meanwhile some attention went also to the problem of rebuilding primary religious schools. No Jew, in 1924, could be content with the situation in Poland and in Eastern Europe, but at least a start had been made toward improvement.

The Communist regime complicated all efforts of assistance in the Soviet Union. At first it was hard even to get in. Harry Fisher and Max Pine persuaded the Estonian government in April, 1920, to permit relief to move through its territory and in June induced the Soviet authorities to accept help. But practical difficulties were insurmountable, and for months thereafter the only aid that reached the Jews in White Russia and the Ukraine was indirect, through the Society of Friends.

The catastrophic crop failures and famine forced the Reds to ease their attitude. A succession of agreements in Riga, Washington and London between August and October, 1921, permitted the JDC to move into Russia under the general auspices of the American Relief Administration, run by Colonel William R. Grove. The Joint contributed $675,000 of its own funds for food and also transmitted $10 packages with life-giving supplies from purchasers in the United States to consumers in the Soviet Union. At one point it was feeding 2,000,000 souls a day. At the same time, it did what it could to further the medical and child care required by 1,500,000 ill and 300,000 Jewish orphans.

In the middle of 1922, the Joint was well established in Russia and operating independently. The moving spirit in the effort was Dr. Joseph A. Rosen, an agronomist who had come over as JDC representative on the American Relief Administration. Russian-born, Rosen had come to the United States in 1903 and worked on farms in Iowa, Kansas and Nebraska before graduating from the Michigan Agricultural College at the age of twenty-nine. He had developed a new strain of winter rye and had made a reputation for himself by work on seed corn; he also had a great interest in and a deep sympathy for the people he was sent to help. He realized that they would need not only to stave off starvation but also to equip themselves for life in the new society taking form about them. To shift away from trade, they would require either equipment with industrial skills or help in transferring their activities to the soil.

Toward the end of that year he persuaded the reconstruction committee of the JDC, of which Herbert H. Lehman was chairman, to allocate $1,290,000 to his efforts. Some of these funds would go to the customary loan funds and vocational training activities, but the largest part was destined for agriculture: for livestock, seeds and tractors, to help the Jews leave the *shtetl* for a new life on the land. With the aid of Dr. Bernhard Kahn, chairman of the Joint's European Executive Council, Rosen brought ten squads with 86 tractors to the Soviet Union the next year and set to work encouraging settlement. In the Crimea he knew there were 6,000,000 empty acres that water, labor and scientific agriculture could redeem.

The experiment went so well that the government and the JDC, on July 21, 1924, created the American Jewish Joint Agricultural Corporation to take over the task under Rosen's direction. Here too was a basis for hope; a large part of the Jewish population were on the way to becoming normal and self-supporting. A cheerful estimate that year showed that the number dependent on trade had declined to a little over 50 per cent from the 70 per cent of 1918. With ORT carrying forward the job of industrial education, and with a revived OSE once more responsible for medical help, the ultimate withdrawal of the JDC from this area was within sight.

Concentration upon the problems of Eastern Europe did not deprive peripheral areas of attention. In 1918, for instance, the journalist Herman Bernstein called the Joint's attention to the desperate condition of the Jews in Siberia —100,000 of them refugees from the West, 10,000 of them taken prisoner from the Austrian Army. Without means of support, victimized by Admiral Kolchak's White army, these helpless people were yielding up their lives by the hundreds each day. A Far East branch, hastily set up in Vladivostok, cooperated with the Siberian War Prisoners Repatriation Fund to rescue the survivors.

Zionist organizations bore the major responsibility for work in Palestine. But the Joint contributed to efforts on behalf of orphans and to medical aid; the malaria research unit it sponsored achieved significant results. There was even an attempt, through the Pro-Falasha committee, to bring some assistance to the long-forgotten Jews of Abyssinia.

By 1924 it was possible to think of winding up the JDC effort. One of its publications that year looked "forward to the moment when its relief work for war sufferers" would "come to an end." It had by then spent more than $62,000,000 in 41 countries and for the first time had brought together in the common task of mercy American Jews of all shades of opinion. But the need had subsided. There was a decline not only in the level of expenditures but also in fund raising. The problems that had brought the Joint into existence were far from solved, but they seemed manageable. It would be a shock, shortly, to learn that they were as grave as ever.

But the experience of these years had developed an organization and had recruited dedicated personnel. After 1920 an accounting and auditing system set up by the firm of Loeb and Troper controlled expenditures, and there was an effort to plan budgets that would make it unnecessary to respond in haste to each alarm. A small but adaptable staff of diverse background and experience brought together a corps of experts ready to take on additional assignments. A network of affiliated Jewish organizations was prepared to assume responsibility for reconstruction, but was also available in the event of unexpected crisis. In 1924 the Joint looked forward to dissolution but was ready to shoulder whatever new problems a disorderly world would present it.

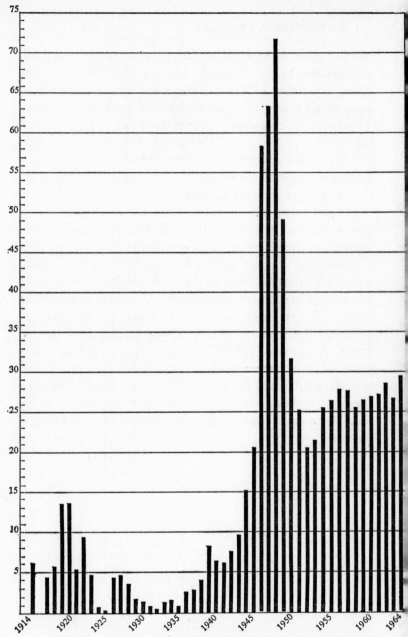

THE AMERICAN JEWISH JOINT DISTRIBUTION COMMITTEE
Income from Oct. 1914 through Dec. 31, 1964 (estimated)
(Figures at left represent millions of dollars.)

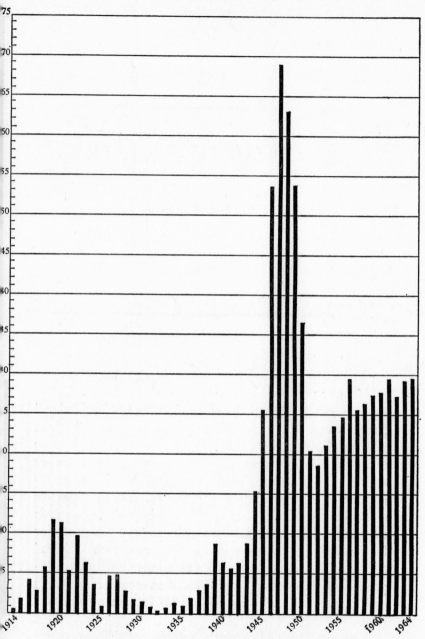

THE AMERICAN JEWISH JOINT DISTRIBUTION COMMITTEE
Expenditures from Oct. 1914 through Dec. 31, 1964 (estimated)
(Figures at left represent millions of dollars.)

IV

ECONOMIC CRISIS

1925-1932

In 1925 the JDC seemed well on the way to "liquidation." Sarajevo was now a decade behind; peace was established, albeit uneasily; and the national boundaries of Europe seemed fixed. Outbreaks of violence—in 1926 at Kishinev and in 1927 at Oradea Mare, both in Rumania—were reminders that anti-Semitism still existed. But its virulence seemed to be subsiding; in 1926 it was possible to conclude that under Pilsudski's new government "the prospects for better times for the Jews of Poland appear to be bright." It was only necessary therefore to arrange an orderly disposition of the assets and functions of an organization which had, in the last analysis, been set up for emergency war relief.

Problems remained, some the products of the war, others

derived from the unhappy prewar heritage of the Jews. But it seemed reasonable to expect that new agencies and new methods would evolve to deal with those long-term difficulties.

The operations of the JDC in the next eight years reflected this dominant assumption. It continued to perform the work at hand, but it also looked hopefully ahead to the moment of its dissolution.

The needs of the refugees, for instance, had shrunk. The moving populations had come to rest, unhappily in many cases, but nevertheless permanently—or so it seemed. The barriers to migration in both the United States and Europe were simply insurmountable. It was a "mockery to talk about emigration," Joseph Rosen pointed out in 1925. The United Evacuation Committee, formed by the Joint and ICA in that year, assumed the responsibility for the few remaining fugitives in transit. But the mass of the Jews would have to adapt themselves to the situation as it was in the countries of their residence. Americans could do no more than help them in the process.

Unfortunately, economic conditions in Eastern Europe did not remain stable long enough to permit the Jews to adjust. A prolonged depression swept across the region after 1925; the economic collapse affected the whole population adversely and created unexpected burdens for the JDC.

It was ironic to speak of depression in an area that was chronically poverty-stricken. Poland, Rumania, Sub-Carpathian Czechoslovakia and Hungary, even in relatively prosperous years contained a distressing number of unemployed poor, who survived only with public assistance. Yet their situation was susceptible to still further deterioration.

In 1925 the creaky productive system began to disintegrate. Crop failures were the immediate cause in Bessarabia and elsewhere, but their impact was so disastrous because the region was already weakened by the consequences of the peace. Poland and Germany plunged into an economic war that damaged them both, and the smaller nationalistic states, cut off from each other by artificial barriers, were unable to sustain a workable economy. In the winter of 1925–26, 83 per cent of the Jewish workers in Warsaw—and half of those in all Poland—were unemployed. There was but slight improvement thereafter. In 1931 the European chairman of the Joint reported that he had never seen such a state of despair as then existed there. In Sub-Carpathian Czechoslovakia, in Rumania and in Hungary the situation was almost as bad as in Poland.

As the decade drew to a close, the signs of breakdown moved steadily toward Central and Western Europe. In 1929 the failure to establish an Austro-German customs union, because of opposition by France and England, brought the depression to the middle of the Continent. The collapse of the Kreditanstalt in Vienna diffused its effects farther west. By the end of that year, securities markets had collapsed in the West and even in the United States. Factories began to shut down, agricultural commodities could find no markets, and the lines of unemployed men lengthened throughout the world. The breakdown would last, in one form or another, until the renewed outbreak of war in 1939. Only the Soviet Union seemed exempt from the effects of depression; whether it actually was or not was hidden from outsiders. In any case, its problems in those years were of another sort.

In the United States and in Western Europe, Jews shared the fate of the rest of the population. In the East, their situation was unique: they suffered disproportionately and yet were not accorded the relief their neighbors received. Year by year, their plight became more perilous.

The JDC quickly felt the effects. It had all along held in view the prospect of eventual liquidation, for it had "never contemplated the replacement of the Jewish leadership existing in the various countries by an improvised system of American relief distributors." Yet Felix Warburg, returning from a European trip in the spring of 1925, decided that the time had not yet come to end its work; year after year thereafter the observers who followed confirmed the same melancholy conclusion.

The European Jewish communities, weakened by economic change and ideologically divided, were less capable of helping themselves than ever before, while the demands on their resources rose frighteningly. With desperate urgency they turned overseas for the aid that had served them in the decade since 1914.

In 1925 Warburg announced that it was "imperative to make an appeal to the Jewish public of the United States for the collection of an adequate fund, which is to be regarded as an overseas chest." That fund could provide for reconstruction, for the care of orphans, for the relief of refugees and for the "urgent problems of sanitation, education and certain other requirements." Such a chest would obviate the need for a multitude of special appeals. He explained that it was "not planned to re-establish the machinery which the Joint Distribution Committee found it necessary to maintain during the war" and that "the funds secured will be disbursed through existing approved agencies."

In September of that year, a conference in Philadelphia launched a single $15,000,000 United Jewish Campaign

under the leadership of David A. Brown. The times, however, were not propitious. The income of the Joint had declined steadily since 1922; in 1925 it amounted to just
about $200,000. The habit of giving had weakened through
disuse. In 1926, 1927 and 1928, strenuous efforts raised
some $12,500,000, and a surplus carried over from previous
years permitted the agency to respond to the demands
made upon it. Some of the organizations it had helped
create also raised additional funds. But when the Depression
affected the United States, the capacity of Americans to
contribute diminished and income sank sharply, declining
from $3,500,000 in 1928 to $380,000 in 1932. Although the
Joint was able to spend more than $18,000,000 in the period
as a whole, its expeditures in 1932 had fallen to their lowest
level in its history. Constricted budgets, which reflected
the erroneous assumption that its work was over, hampered
its efforts in this period of transition.

The structure and staff of the agency remained much
as it had been in 1924. Felix M. Warburg, Herbert H.
Lehman and James N. Rosenberg were the leaders most involved in its administration. Paul Baerwald, a New York
banker, bore the responsibilities of treasurer, and Rabbi
Jonah B. Wise, of New York's Central Synagogue, supplied spiritual counsel and speaking ability in place of
Judah L. Magnes, who had gone to Palestine.

In 1925 the Joint did acquire the services of a professional
administrator to lend continuity to the efforts of its lay
leaders. Joseph C. Hyman was born in Sycrause in 1889
and had been educated at Columbia University and the
New York Law School. He had been a high school teacher
and had briefly practiced law, but during the war had
been drawn into Jewish social work. In 1922 he became
Lehman's assistant, handling the details of the work of the
reconstruction committee; three years later he became

secretary of the JDC. For almost two decades thereafter he bore a major share of the responsibility for its labors.

With no sharp break in direction, the JDC was inclined to rely upon the usual procedures of the past in dealing with the problems of Eastern Europe. Since it had no political aims, it had to assume that it would not be able to alter the economic and social systems of the countries in which it worked. It could only strive to adjust the Jews to the status quo. It did not wish to extend a perpetual dole to the chronically dependent, but rather to make the population productive and self-supporting. To do so it had to aid the artisans and tradesmen in establishing themselves. In the midst of a great depression, that was a wellnigh impossible assignment.

There was no escaping the problems of the homeless, the hungry and the orphaned. Some charges for their relief remained on the Joint budget. In 1926 aid still went to 14,000 orphans in 300 Polish communities through the Central Children's Committee in Warsaw. But there was a consistent effort to divert an ever larger percentage of resources from palliative to constructive aid.

The struggle, by then more than a half century old, to equip East European Jews with handicraft skills continued. The Joint cooperated with ICA and ORT in support of vocational training and derived encouragement from each indication that the traditional Jew was turning into a laborer. When a carpentry shop appeared in the *yeshiva* at Iclod in Transylvania, that seemed a significant indication of change, a basis for hope that manual work would become a conventional part of Orthodox life.

To acquire a skill was one thing, to find a market for it another, particularly in hostile societies which excluded the Jew from their cooperatives, and in which state monopolies often made him the victim of boycotts. Occasional Jewish producers' and consumers' cooperatives aimed to strengthen the economic position of handworkers. But, as earlier, great reliance was placed on the credit *kassa*, or loan cooperative, which was expected to get the small merchant or artisan on his feet. In 1926, 300 such organizations with 85,000 members were affiliated with the Central Cooperative Bank in Warsaw; five years later 760 *kassas* in Poland, Austria, Bulgaria, Czechoslovakia, Rumania, Turkey, Latvia, Lithuania and Estonia held $11,750,000 in deposits and made $60,000,000 in loans to their 325,000 members. Most of them had been set up with the aid of the American Joint Reconstruction Foundation, the legatee of the JDC in this field.

To meet the needs of the poorest, who could not become members of a *kassa*, the Joint set out, in 1926, to revitalize the traditional *gemilath chesed*, or free loan societies, matching local contributions for their support. By 1931 Poland alone had more than 600 such organizations, which served 100,000 clients annually.

Faith in the recuperative value of medicine and education also endured. Aid continued to go to OSE for its work on behalf of health throughout the region; and regular subventions to nurses training schools, to teachers seminaries and to *yeshivoth* reflected the hope that perhaps the future, at least, would improve. The bitter conflicts which divided Orthodox from secular Jews, Yiddishists from Hebraists, and Zionists from nationalists were not resolved but compromised by shifting the responsibility for decisions to the local communities in the hope that they would somehow be able to work matters out peaceably for themselves.

The Soviet Union, which in the 1920's contained some 2,750,000 Jews, stood in a special category. It was cut off from the rest of the world, so that accurate information about its development was difficult to come by, particularly in the United States, which had no diplomatic relations with it. Since the Communist regime exercised strict control over its minority populations, relatively little was known about the fate of the Jews except that many of them were now moving to such large cities as Leningrad and Moscow.

An exceptionally favorable impression of Soviet society spread about the world. It was true that the Joint had some difficulty in continuing its support of cultural institutions in the face of antireligious disapproval; the Habimah Theater was thus forced to leave in 1926 because Hebrew was considered a counterrevolutionary language. But the Landsmannschaft Bureau in New York, through the JDC, was able to aid rabbis in hundreds of Russian towns.

Above all, the new system had, it appeared, ended depressions; its fortunate citizens did not suffer as did those of capitalist countries. Futhermore, the claim that it had by law abolished anti-Semitism and had ended the discriminatory practices of the czarist past won it the sympathy of Jews who knew all too well the hardships of the earlier regime and who had no way of assessing the rosy estimate the new order gave of itself. Here there seemed a genuine prospect for a reconstruction of Jewish life, particularly in the one area in which the Soviet government encouraged outside assistance, the furtherance of agricultural settlement.

At last, after centuries of exclusion, the Jews were to have access to the soil, to the immemorial dream of living as normal men, each under his own vine and fig tree. In October, 1926, a Joint representative saw the Jews come across the miles and miles of endless Russian steppes, where a person could be lost as easily as a canoe on the ocean.

They were opening a new chapter in their history. They were coming back to the soil.

Dr. Rosen's enthusiasm, the encouragement of the Soviet government and American support would redeem them from their past. Exposed to nature, they would lose the attributes of the ghetto dweller. "The eugenic value of having a large number of our co-religionists get out into God's sunshine once more to earn their bread by the sweat of their brow" would make new and different men of them. The pallid, chronically ill *lishentzy*—the vocational drifters of the cities—weak from lack of occupation, would turn into strong and healthy yeomen, thereby strengthening family life and religion. Anti-Semitism would disappear and pogroms would be recalled only in the record of past barbarisms. The experiment would therefore point the direction of the future solution of the Jewish problem everywhere. "A Russian-Jewish peasantry will powerfully influence the governmental policies of other European lands with respect to our fellow Jews." That was the hope as the 1920's drew to an end.

The Agro-Joint, created in 1924, worked closely with the Soviet agency, KOMZET (Commission for the Rural Placement of Jewish Toilers), to get the settlers to the land in the Ukraine and Crimea. The hopeful pioneers first went out in the spring of 1925. It cost between $750 and $1,000 to establish a household, of which sum the Agro-Joint contributed one third. By the fall of 1926 it had expended $2,400,000 and had helped about 10,000 families. At the start the newcomers were organized in collectives, but it was expected that they would ultimately disperse onto individual holdings. At the end of 1927, Dr. Rosen estimated that 35,000 Jewish families were tilling the Russian soil, and before the next year was over the JDC had contributed almost $6,000,000 to help them do so.

By then it was time to devise a permanent system for aiding the enterprise. The Joint leaders established the American Society for Jewish Farm Settlements in Russia, with James Rosenberg as chairman and with Warburg, Baerwald, Lehman and Marshall among the directors. An energetic drive for support yielded $8,000,000, of which $5,000,000 came from Julius Rosenwald; $1,000,000 from Warburg; and $500,000 from John D. Rockefeller, Jr. The Soviet Union made the land available and contributed an equal sum to create a capital fund for sustaining the process of settlement.

The Agro-Joint helped individual farmers, but was particularly interested in establishing new colonies. It encouraged groups to form; aided in the selection and survey of sites; dug wells; rented tractors; made loans for seed and stock; provided medical services; and supplied agronomists to instruct would-be husbandmen, who at first "did not know how to harness a horse, how to handle a plow." The number so established on the soil increased until 1933, although at a diminishing rate, which indicated that the high hopes held for the project would not soon be fulfilled.

Other Russian Jews were not forgotten. Joint aid still went in declining amounts to credit *kassas*, to mutual-aid societies, to cooperatives and to trade schools. Collaboration also continued with ORT, ICA and OSE in reconstruction and medical activities. But the greatest hopes fastened upon the development of the Jewish agriculturist. The JDC leaders could not know that by 1928 the Communist Party of the Soviet Union had already decided to turn against these projects and to push the proletarianization of the Jews. In view of its trouble with the kulaks it had no desire to increase the number of peasants. The consequences of that decision would only emerge later; for the time being it was possible still to look ahead optimistically.

. . .

Another face of the future was becoming apparent after 1925 in Palestine. The Jewish community there had grown since the organization of the mandate government to an extent that encouraged a group around Julian W. Mack and Louis D. Brandeis to create the Palestine Economic Corporation in 1926. This autonomous enterprise, headed by Bernard Flexner, was thereafter to assume primary responsibility for economic development on a businesslike basis. The Joint encouraged the venture with a grant of some $1,800,000. The corporation also took over the existing JDC loan *kassa* program and went on to set up banking, mortgage and water companies designed to further development. The re-organization of the Jewish Agency in 1929 to make room for non-Zionist members also offered a means for assistance that promised to reduce the task of the Joint. While the JDC still spent some $1,300,000 in the Holy Land for such existing commitments as aid to immigrants and to cultural institutions, it could properly expect that the demands on it would decline and ultimately vanish.

But a depression hit the country in 1927, and two years later, organized Arab riots caused severe damage and induced the British authorities to adopt the policies of the Passfield White Paper, which sharply restricted future immigration. Here too, a Jewish organization could make plans, work hard to implement them and yet find them frustrated by power over which it had no control.

Year by year, from 1925 to 1933, the reports of the JDC were couched in encouraging terms, despite the gloomy news they often had to convey. Its agents emphasized positive achievements; they could see the good they were doing —the lives they saved, the health they restored, the hope they instilled. They freely sacrificed themselves for a vision that was worth cherishing, of a people reborn out of the pangs of war and able to live in peace, dignity and equality among their neighbors. The JDC could have done no better than it did.

In retrospect, however, it is clear that nothing done for the Jews alone would have been adequate to forestall the disasters yet to come. The Jews were part of a larger society, whose fate would determine their own. The economic depression was a symptom of Europe's inner illness. The Joint could ameliorate the pathologic effects upon the Jews; it could not reach the heart of the disease which shortly would alter the character of the whole world, of Jews as of others.

V

THE SCOURGE OF

NAZISM

1933–1939

In January, 1933, the corruption that had long been fester-ing within European society emerged to the surface; for the next seven years it spread until war once more engulfed the Continent. This time there would be no recovery for many parts of that world.

Central and Eastern Europe had never regained their strength after 1918. The debilitating economic disorganiza-tion of the 1920's became even more oppressive after 1930. In the East, only Czechoslovakia retained a semblance of demo-cratic government in 1933; elsewhere dictatorship had been the response to social tension.

In Germany, depression deepened the damage caused by the loss of the war. Reparations and inflation sapped the strength of the middle classes, and an army of unemployed, drained of hope, grew desperate as its grievances remained unredressed. The mass of unattached men formed a combustible element in the population, seeking some cause to which to attach themselves. The Communists offered one extreme way out; their open revolt had failed but they retained a substantial following. Only their internationalism and their ties to the Soviet Union limited their popular appeal.

Another extremist movement was growing steadily more attractive. The German National Socialist Party preached both socialism and nationalism and offered its adherents, in addition, the consolation of a mystical racial unity. The brown-shirted ritual restored pride in their Aryan identity to men who could only respect themselves if they had an inferior folk to look down upon. In 1932 the Nazis were the largest political group in Germany.

In that year the Weimar Republic had already ceased to function effectively. The ruling Center Party had taken to governing by decree rather than by parliamentary action and it had finally yielded office to a succession of weak conservative administrations. In the mounting crisis, President Von Hindenburg and Franz von Papen, who spoke for the Junkers, the Army and the great industrialists and who feared above all the Red menace in the East, thought that they could make the Nazis their tools. With their connivance Adolf Hitler, who had never secured a majority vote of the German electorate, came to power as chancellor in a coalition government.

Within two months he had swept away the Reichstag and every other restraint and had made himself sole master of the country. The opposition melted away as the more stubborn were ruthlessly liquidated and the more submissive were cowed. Soon a series of impressive gains abroad showed the extent of Nazi power. Hitler remilitarized the Rhineland in disregard of every treaty provision; he seized Austria, took the Sudetenland and then made all of Czechoslovakia a protectorate in a dramatic demonstration of the rewards of the naked use of force.

The great Western powers stood idly by as the Führer flouted the last vestiges of international law. The concessions they had refused to the democratic Weimar Republic in diplomatic negotiations they allowed the dictator Hitler to grasp by terror. At first their own cynicism misled them. Fascism in Italy, Hungary and Poland they had regarded as an eccentricity useful for preserving order and for halting the spread of Communism; they thought the Nazi variety would be the same. None therefore mourned the failure of democracy in Germany; none took the blustering Austrian house-painter seriously. And when Hitler gathered the reins of power in his own hands no one moved to halt him. His deluded neighbors allowed him to build his great Third Reich without hindrance. "Why die for Danzig?" too many asked while Hitler finally readied his campaign against Poland in his drive toward the East.

Earlier in the 1930's, impressive achievements in foreign policy strengthened the hand of the Nazis at home. Their efforts to eliminate the Jews from German life met no serious resistance. It soon became apparent that Hitler's racial theories were not merely harmless idiosyncrasies or devices for consolidating power. He took seriously the dogmas of Aryan purity and superiority and he was in deadly earnest in his threats against the Jewish folk enemies. Step by step he moved along a course that made literally true the incredible predictions in *Mein Kampf*. The German people willingly followed and the rest of the world had neither the will nor the ability to intervene.

The persecution of 600,000 Jews in Germany proceeded with relentless logic. Anyone with even one Jewish grandparent, and therefore legally defined as non-Aryan, was immediately dismissed from all public offices and from the universities. Barred from membership in professional organizations, such people were unable to practice law or medicine. Nazi pressure and popular boycotts forced the Aryanization of many business enterprises. Excluded from the trade unions, the Jews were unable to find industrial employment. Meanwhile, terror softened the opposition and increased the difficulties of the victims. The flow of prisoners into the concentration camps started almost at once and mounted steadily, year by year. The Nuremberg decrees of September, 1935, established the permanent inferiority of the Jews' status; and the pogrom of the "Crystal Night" in 1938 exposed them to continuing acts of terrorism. By that year the number subject to Nazi oppression had grown tragically, for the conquest of Austria had brought the 190,000 Jewish nationals of that country also within the range of Hitlerite rule.

The Jews were too few in number, too poorly organized and too little prepared to be able to defend themselves. They had considered themselves well adjusted, totally integrated in the society and culture of their fatherland; they counted on their achievements, their respectability and their positions to earn them the support of their fellow citizens. In vain! As the bleak consequences of isolation became apparent, they organized for mutual aid and self-protection. But the choices available to them were meager indeed. Like the humblest Polish or Russian Jew they too now needed help from overseas.

Nothing, meanwhile, had substantially improved the situation in Eastern Europe. The plight of the Jews was as difficult as it had been in the 1920's. In Poland, 1,000,000 of the 3,000,000 had incomes below the subsistence level. Everywhere they were discriminated against in education and employment. Furthermore, Hitler's success gave heart to anti-Semites throughout the region. In 1938, for instance, when the Goga dictatorship was installed in Rumania, it unleashed a reign of terror against the 900,000 Jews in that land. Open violence then brought to public attention a misery that had existed without much notice since the war. In May of that year Hungary imposed a *numerus clausus* on its Jews; in September Italy moved toward a racial policy and expelled 15,000 Jews who had entered the kingdom since 1914. Thus, the poison generated in Germany spread through the Continent. Nowhere east of the Rhine could American Jews in this decade find cause to believe that their co-religionists no longer needed assistance.

The Joint Distribution Committee in 1933 was a permanent organization. Its reports occasionally referred wistfully to a future in which its work would end; but that moment had receded into the remote distance. In its New York office on Hanover Street, Joseph C. Hyman, its secretary, and his assistants Evelyn M. Morrissey and Dorothy L. Speiser kept informed of developments in Europe and maintained contact with the agencies that had been expected to carry on the long-range tasks of reconstruction. Meanwhile, Kahn, Rosen and David J. Schweitzer remained the Joint representatives in Europe. There was substantial continuity in the lay leadership also: Paul Baerwald had replaced Felix Warburg (in 1937) as chief executive and Louis Marshall had died in 1929, but much the same families were represented on the Board in 1939 as in 1914.

The events in Germany now heightened the sense of responsibility that had all along moved these men. They had had particularly close ties—of kinship and of culture—with that country and they felt a personal sense of loss as it slipped into barbarism. The urge to help was strong; the problem was—how?

The Joint, then as always, abjured any political role and left to others the tasks of protest and mediation. It disliked Hitler but it had to accept the status quo. Its task was relief.

Therein it differed in emphasis from the Zionists, who were convinced that every energy ought to be focused upon the settlements in Palestine. The Joint leaders did not wish to disregard the present in the interests of the future, nor could they assume that immediate needs would be satisfied, under existing conditions, by counseling emigration to the Holy Land. Some tension between the two viewpoints persisted down to 1939.

The crisis of 1933 called for an accommodation, however. JDC income had been declining precipitously since 1929, and experience showed that an increased demand for funds was likely; in the midst of the Depression it was imperative that collections be as efficient as possible and that potential contributors not be plagued by a multitude of campaigns. On March 11, 1934, therefore, Baerwald and representatives of the Jewish Agency for Palestine agreed on a United Jewish Appeal to raise $3,000,000, to be allocated equitably between the two bodies. Although the trial did not satisfy everyone and the experiment was dropped in 1936, 1937 and 1938, some such association was inevitable. When the war clouds gathered once more, there was a basis for future fund-raising collaboration.

From their low point in 1932, Joint expenditures began to rise steadily, if slowly. They did not, in this period, regain the level of the 1920's, but in 1938 $4,000,000 was budgeted, and the agency was ready for the still larger requirements that would develop in 1939 and later. In all, it spent nearly $12,000,000 in these years.

. . .

In April, 1933, Rabbi Jonah B. Wise went to Germany on behalf of the JDC. There he helped organize the Zentral Ausschuss für Hilfe und Aufbau, through which the Jews of that country hoped to coordinate and administer aid on their own behalf. Subcommittees were charged with responsibility for emigration, economic relief, social service and fund raising and were to coordinate their efforts with the Joint, which shifted its European headquarters from Berlin to Paris but maintained an office in the German capital.

The desire to escape was strong, but the ties to home, to careers and to associates were not easily severed. Richard Willstäter, the Nobel Prize chemist who had always maintained his Jewish identification, knew that Germany had gone mad. But he could not tear himself away. "If a mother falls ill it is not a reason for her children to leave her. My home is Germany, my university, in spite of what has happened, is in Munich." To depart under such circumstances was to yield to the Nazis, to acknowledge that they were right in the belief that there was no place for the Jews in Germany. Men like Willstäter recognized the danger only late and with reluctance.

The first to go were the aliens who indeed had no choice, for they were simply expelled. Foreign-born Jews were deprived of their German citizenship and also forced to migrate along with such natives as foresaw the consequences of staying. By the end of 1933, some 30,000 had left the Reich.

The times were not favorable for migration, however. To move was expensive, and even the individuals with money could not readily turn it into convertible currency. Furthermore, there was literally no place to go. Europe and America were still in the depths of depression and no country was willing to receive even small additions to its population. The Jews were being crushed between the Nazi pressure on them to leave and the stone wall of regulations that prevented their entry elsewhere.

The League of Nations, conscious of the international implications of the problem and desirous of finding a solution, in December, 1933, created a High Commission for Refugees under James G. McDonald. But little came of his efforts. In 1935 he resigned, with the warning that philanthropic action would not end the difficulties in the Reich and that a "terrible human calamity'" would result in the absence of outside governmental help. Yet the thirty-two nations which conferred at Evian in July, 1938, at the invitation of the United States, made only token gestures toward easing the dilemma of the fugitives, whom no one wanted and for whom no one felt responsible.

The Joint did what it could. It contributed to the High Commissioner's budget, and it arranged a system by which refugees could leave their money in Germany for local aid in exchange for dollars to help them on their way, so that the Nazis would not profit from their departure. It cooperated with the Central British Fund in the tasks of salvage as the problems of the decade deepened. Assistance from the Joint helped the Vienna community meet the crisis of Anschluss, and subventions enabled HICEM, an emigrant aid organization in which ICA and HIAS participated, to work with the Jews who got out from Germany, Austria and Czechoslovakia. In France, Switzerland and the Low Countries, where many found refuge, the Joint had to sustain local efforts to keep the newcomers from becoming public charges, for that might have closed the remaining routes of escape. For the same reason it was vital to help those who arrived in Latin America to establish themselves.

These efforts saved thousands of lives. More than 100,000 Jews had left Germany by the end of 1935, and 260,000 by the end of 1939, in addition to 124,000 from Austria and 43,000 from Czechoslovakia. But the great majority then still remained imprisoned in the areas of Nazi control.

The people who could not escape, it was clear, "would perforce have to readjust their lives within Germany itself, there seek new occupations, and train their youth for new callings." The JDC, along with the British and French Jews, contributed substantially for that purpose to the budget of the Zentral Ausschuss. By 1937 almost one third of the German Jews depended upon aid. There were efforts at vocational retraining to help the non-Aryans earn their living under difficult conditions. The organization made loans to keep the desperate from going under and also served as custodian of enterprises to prevent capital from falling into the hands of the state. It undertook a program of child care and set up a school system to compensate for the public education of which Jewish children had been deprived. In 1937, 23,670 children were enrolled in 167 such institutions. By then an anomalous, self-contained community in German lands lived largely by consuming its capital and by aid from the United States. Excluded from productive callings, heavily taxed yet barred from any governmental benefits or institutions, exposed to violence and to legal discrimination, the Jews faced a future of bleak dependence.

Nazism cast a shadow across all of Eastern Europe. Even where the Germans did not yet rule, there was no improvement in a situation which had been bad enough in 1933. In that year one half of all Polish Jews were destitute; and through the American Joint Reconstruction Foundation the JDC was helping 300,000 breadwinners in the region as a whole. Loan societies of various types numbered over 900 by the end of the period, and the valiant efforts to raise the standards of medical and child care persisted.

To think ahead in this decade was to open up violently divisive issues among the Jews of both Europe and America. The mounting threat of Fascism did not unite its potential victims; rather, the danger drew their attention to competing programs. Zionism, socialism, assimilationism, nationalism—each sect had its devoted advocates. It was only in such practical work as the Joint undertook that common effort was at all possible, for in these matters the needs of the moment were so great that there was no time to wonder: To what ultimate end?

Until the disillusionment of the Hitler-Stalin pact in 1939 there seemed cause for optimism about developments in the Soviet Union. Down to Munich, the Communist leaders remained sensitive to world opinion, for they then pursued the policy of the united front against Fascism and posed as the defenders of all victims of oppression. They were relatively tolerant therefore of KOMZET's activities on behalf of Jewish economic development, not only of those administered directly in the autonomous state of Birobidzhan but also of those in the Ukraine and Crimea in which the Agro-Joint participated. In 1933 that agency, with JDC support, had aided the settlement of some 35,000 families, and its work continued for another five years.

In 1938 a network of loan and mutual-aid societies assisted the productive; 42 schools offered training in trade and agriculture; and 63 organizations furthered medical services—all with the direct or indirect assistance of the Joint and its subsidiaries. In that year also, more than 250,000 Jewish farmers were said to be tilling some 3,000,000 acres in Russia. These figures were undoubtedly inflated, for the Soviet census a year later counted only 175,000 Jews in agriculture in the whole country.

Which calculation was the more accurate had lost importance by then; in 1938 the Soviet government completed the dissolution of all the Jewish institutions with foreign connections, ostensibly because they had fulfilled their purpose. However, the Birobidzhan leaders were liquidated and KOMZET was closed down at just about the same time—facts which indicated that other forces were involved. The great purges that followed the "Trotskyite" trials of 1937, the abandonment of the united front, the tightening of the state apparatus and anticipation of the shift in Party line that was to come in August, 1939—all contributed to the end of Joint work in Russia. It was no doubt just as well that American Jews for the moment were spared the foreknowledge of what was shortly to happen.

These were also years of steady deterioration in the situation in Palestine. In 1933 this had been one of the few areas of the world open to the refugees from Germany; increasingly the flow of migration moved in that direction, often supported by Joint resources. The Palestine Economic Corporation also remained active in developing the economic basis for expanding settlement.

But that very growth increased the hostility of the Arabs, who were fearful of becoming a minority in the land of their birth. In April, 1936, the nationalist Arab Higher Committee led a general strike, a boycott of Jewish business and a civil disobedience campaign in protest. Sabotage and violence followed, and then sporadic guerrilla warfare. A British Royal Commission investigated, and in July, 1937, reported that an irrepressible and irreconcilable conflict existed between Arabs and Jews. It therefore suggested a restriction of immigration. After almost two years of delay, the mandatory power finally announced its policy. It would allow 75,000 Jews to enter in the next five years, but thereafter further admissions would require Arab consent. At about the same time it suspended all immigration for six months in reprisal for illegal entries by refugees. That was in July, 1939. Before the six months were over, the world had changed.

In its handling of the Palestine question the English government had not taken account of the actualities of Nazi power. But then, no government had—in Europe or in America. Without interference Hitler was free to prepare the calamity McDonald had predicted. For seven years his ruthless hatred of the Jews had created problems with which the Joint wrestled to the best of its ability. The worst was yet to come.

VI

WAR AGAIN

1939-1945

IN THE BELEAGUERED WARSAW GHETTO, the archivist Emmanuel Ringelblum noted that everyone was keeping diaries: ". . . journalists and writers, of course, but also teachers, public men, young people—even children." The wish somehow to preserve a record reflected the desperate insistence that the incredible events of the moment must have a meaning, though what it was, was not clear for the time being.

So too, in November, 1941, twenty-two Jewish doctors confined to that same ghetto undertook a scientific study. Since clinical materials were abundant, they decided to investigate the influence of famine upon the human organism. Each team took a distinct phase of the subject and worked industriously; time was short. Unfortunately, they could not be as precise as they wished; deportation and death cut off their labor. David Guzik, of the Joint, found their manuscript after the war, but he too died before it was finally published in 1946. The calm words of the text and the objectivity of the pictures reveal that the doctors too sought a meaning. It was as if they strove, in the last moments of fading hope, to bequeath at least some understanding to posterity.

A quarter of a century later it remains difficult to unravel the meaning in these events. For each individual of the millions involved there was a different story.

Joseph Robitschek, a ceramics engineer in Czechoslovakia, flees to Belgium in 1939 when the Germans come. In June of the following year, that refuge is invaded; he sets off for France with his wife and young daughter. The Wehrmacht follows. In Marseilles he acquires a Portuguese visa and then slips across the Pyrenees after once being turned back by Spanish border guards. He is fortunate, gets to Lisbon, acquires a Brazilian visa, and with several hundred other refugees sets sail for Rio in January, 1941, on the French steamer *Alsina*. At sea, the vessel is turned back by the Vichy government. After five months on board in the harbor at Dakar, the Robitscheks are interned at Casablanca. At last a Spanish ship takes them to Rio, but they are refused permission to land and finally come ashore at Curaçao. There an American visa is available and also passage on a Dutch freighter. They are torpedoed in the Caribbean, rescued, then torpedoed again and at last disembark in Colon—but without their precious papers. After repeated delays they ultimately get to the United States.

The meaning of this case is simple. There were two requirements for the Robitscheks' survival—luck, and also some representative of the Joint to deal with their problems at every point they touched in their wanderings. But the hundreds of thousands of such cases, in the aggregate, are not so easy to understand.

. . .

The war started in miscalculation. Having reached an agreement with Stalin, Hitler assumed that the Western powers would no more honor their guarantees to the Poles than they had to the Czechs. He was wrong. The cost of that error was the destruction of his Reich and almost six years of total war.

For the first nine months all went well. The two dictators divided Poland, and the West remained quiet. Then came the swift attack upon Denmark, Norway, the Low Countries and France, after which, for a year, only Britain held off a German victory. The war reached a new stage of intensity in 1941, when Hitler turned upon the Russians and when Japanese attacks in the Far East brought the United States into the conflict. Almost four years of destruction followed until the Axis powers were finally defeated.

In this conflict the Jews suffered, as did the inhabitants of all the belligerent countries. In addition, their abnormal situation in Eastern Europe left them unprotected, as it had in the First World War. And now they encountered the iron determination of the Nazi Führer to eliminate them, by one means or another, from the life of Europe. In 1939 Hitler had informed the Reichstag: "If the international Jewish financiers inside and outside Europe should again succeed in plunging the nations into a world war, the result will be not the Bolshevization of the earth and thus the victory of Jewry, but the annihilation of the Jewish race throughout Europe." He was almost to make good this mad boast.

The fate of the Jews everywhere depended upon the character of the government under which they lived and upon its relationship to the occupying power. The first test of direct German rule came in Poland, where the conquerors determined to use the Jews in industry insofar as their manpower was helpful, and then to eliminate them by expulsion or extermination. To that end the refugees who had fled from the countryside were kept in the cities, and after October, 1940, all Jews were confined to ghettos. In Warsaw, 80,000 Christians moved out of, and 150,000 Jews were driven into, a walled-in area of about a thousand acres that was to shelter, at its peak, some 450,000 souls. In the first year, starvation and typhus took more than 56,000 victims and the toll mounted thereafter. Meanwhile, in the East the Soviet authorities were not openly anti-Semitic, but they crushed all existing communal organizations in their zone. The sinister significance of these measures would appear later.

The beginning of the end came with the German invasion of Russia in June, 1941. The Nazi armies sliced eastward deep into the Ukraine with the aid of their new allies in Hungary, Bulgaria and Rumania. With them went special killing squads and mobile gas trucks which quickly disposed of 600,000 victims. (Only one survivor could later be found of the colonists established with so much effort by the Agro-Joint in the Ukraine and Crimea.) A vast army of refugees fled before the oncoming troops, some moving far beyond the Ural Mountains to Siberia. Through the remainder of that year, Hitler still considered the Jews hostages and madly hoped that the American financiers would ransom them for transportation to Madagascar or some other remote corner of the earth. That delusion vanished after Pearl Harbor. Then, in July, 1942, the deportation trains rolled to the extermination chambers of Auschwitz and Treblinka, carrying the "subhumans" to the "final solution." Soon the ghettos were empty.

Paradoxically, for a time the Jewish subjects of Germany's allies fared better. Hungary and Bulgaria were ruled by cruel dictators, but not by madmen. These governments were willing to listen to reason or, at least, to consult their own self-interest; they maintained a somewhat restraining influence on the Nazis until these territories were occupied in 1944. Then the process of internment, deportation, flight and extermination appeared there too.

The fate of the Rumanian Jews was more complex but no less tragic. Fully 110,000 of the 150,000 in Transylvania lost their lives when that province was transferred to Hungary. During the invasions of Bukovina and Bessarabia, another 100,000 died. And only a small fraction of the 185,000 exiled to Transnistria were ever to come back.

In the jungles of Europe no one was safe. The West suffered, as did the East. As the Wehrmacht occupied the Netherlands, Belgium and France, the fugitives fled southward, some of them already refugees from another migration. For a time Vichy territory was relatively safe, although immigrants who had entered the country after 1936 were interned and the Pétain regime acquiesced in a growing list of anti-Semitic measures. But full German occupation in November, 1942, closed off all hope in France as in the rest of the Continent. The Jews were isolated from the rest of the population, sent to concentration camps as long as their labor was useful, and as soon as it was not, directed to the death chambers. Six million were victims.

In this war there were no illusions either about the magnitude or the duration of the task of relief. The problems of rescue would not be easily or quickly solved. The American Jews bore almost the whole burden. The communities in Europe, in South Africa, England, Latin America and in

Canada did what they could, but the central responsibility now more than ever before rested in the United States, and that meant in the JDC.

The historic program of the Joint offered all Jews a basis for unity of action. Its efforts to aid had always been non-political and humanitarian, based on the assumption that the Jews had a right either to live where they were or to emigrate. Its American insistence on "giving to all an equal opportunity for survival and creative life" was enriched "by the Biblical concept of social obligation and mercy." It could therefore rise above all factional divisions. In 1942 the writer Stefan Zweig explained: "Later, at some future date, we shall again gladly and passionately discuss whether Jews should be Zionists, revisionists, territorialists or assimilationists; we shall discuss the hair-splitting point of whether we are a nation, a religion, a people or a race. All of these time-consuming, theoretical discussions can wait. Now there is but one thing for us to do—to give help."

The Joint was prepared. Its lay leadership shifted to the second generation in February, 1941, when Edward M. M. Warburg, Felix's son, assumed the chairmanship at Baerwald's retirement. Then in his mid-thirties, Warburg had inherited his father's interest both in the fine arts and in philanthropy. A few months after Pearl Harbor, Edward enlisted in the United States Army as a private, but he managed to keep in touch with affairs at the agency and retained a deep sense of involvement in it. Although such family connections persisted, the JDC was also flexible enough to incorporate new elements in the Jewish community and to develop truly national connections throughout the United States. The task these men faced was greater than ever before, but they were more confident than their predecessors had been and therefore more daring, able to think and act on a larger scale.

Policy decisions rested in the hands of the Executive Committee of the Board, which met monthly, and operations proceeded under the supervision of weekly sessions of the Administrative Committee. But volunteers could no longer transact the business of an organization which handled thousands of letters and cables a month and functioned in every part of the world. That took a full-time permanent group of workers.

The professional staff was small but effective and zealous, capable of making the sacrifices and exercising the diplomacy the task demanded. A reorganization of the New York office, now on East 42nd Street, made Hyman executive vice-chairman in 1940 and brought to the operating secretaryship Moses A. Leavitt, then forty-six years old, a graduate of Cornell and a chemical engineer who had left industry to work for the Jewish Social Service Association in 1923. In 1929 he entered the service of the JDC and in 1933 he became secretary of the Palestine Economic Corporation; thus, he was familiar with the Joint's business when he returned to the JDC in 1940.

Across the Atlantic, supervision of the JDC affairs passed from Bernhard Kahn, first to Morris C. Troper and then to Joseph J. Schwartz, who became director-general in 1942. Schwartz had arrived in the United States from Russia in 1907 at the age of eight and after an Orthodox education had become a rabbi. Scholarly interests led him to a doctorate at Yale, but after a brief teaching career he entered social work. He was executive director of the Brooklyn Federation of Jewish Charities when he came to the Joint in 1939. Hyman, Leavitt and he combined talents vital to the success of the enterprise.

Around the world they were able to recruit dedicated staff and volunteer collaborators. Most of the professionals by now were products of social-work training, skilled, experienced and imbued with a sense of mission about their work. The laymen were a heterogeneous group: Saly Mayer, a retired lace manufacturer of St. Gall in Switzerland, who became an indispensable financial intermediary; Moses B. Amzalak, of Lisbon, a scholarly economist who assumed unexpected responsibilities in that vital port of escape; the Kadoorie brothers, bankers in China, suddenly called on to aid.

Within the United States, the Joint developed a network of committees with contacts in some 2,000 local organizations to further its drive for funds. Regional and zonal conferences and attractive publications made its work known everywhere. In the larger cities, by now, federations ran united campaigns and distributed the proceeds; it was necessary to stimulate the JDC's friends in each place, not only to aid in the collections but also to secure an appropriate share of the allocations. On the other hand, pressure came from local sources, and particularly from their spokesmen in the Council of Jewish Federations and Welfare Funds, to consolidate all general overseas campaigns into a single United Jewish Appeal. After 1939 therefore, except for a brief interval in 1941, the Joint collaborated with the Zionists and with the agencies involved in other immigration work in a common effort of solicitation in every corner of the country. In 1942, the call reached 3,975 communities in the United States.

The response was gratifying. American Jews were now, to an increasing extent, native-born and middle-class. Comparing their own security and well-being with the lot of their European co-religionists, they knew that they were not more virtuous or more valuable than the others, only more fortunate. "It is only by accident that we are here and not over there," safe in our own homes rather than fearfully waiting for the fist at the door. People through whose minds these thoughts passed learned to meet the challenge of repeated demands on behalf of those others.

Joint income was sustained at a level of between $6,000,-000 and $15,000,000 a year between 1939 and the end of the war, not enough to meet all needs, just the most pressing. But the Joint was now willing to risk expenditures above receipts, running deficits that rose in 1943 to more than $1,000,000 and trusting to the future to be able to repay obligations to the overseas communities which also borrowed on its credit. In all, in these years it spent $50,850,200.

In the use of these resources, the Joint had to keep in view three separate but related objectives. Aid was essential to keep alive the Jews who lived anywhere under Nazi domination; escape was to be arranged for those who could manage it; and help had to reach immigrants in the countries of refuge to forestall any unfavorable reaction among native citizens.

All this had to be done without putting into German hands any dollars that might assist the enemy war effort. The JDC used for the purpose marks or francs put at its disposal by emigrants lucky enough to get out, and also borrowed from local sources on the promise of postwar repayment. These maneuvers gave it some means for saving the lives of the Nazi victims. In 1941 in Poland alone it administered direct relief in 408 localities to 600,000 individuals and contributed to the support of almost 2,000 institutions.

The Polish ghettos at first attempted to organize their own communal and cultural services, but their resources were pitifully small. Consequently they quickly became dependent on the Joint, which maintained an office in Warsaw until Pearl Harbor. Under the energetic direction of its representatives—Isaac Borenzteyn, Isaac Gitterman, Leon Neu-

sztadt and David Guzik—it mobilized the assistance to keep
the people alive. Soup kitchens for the refugees, doles for
the jobless, trade schools, provision for the orphans and the
ill went into operation with desperate urgency. Supplies
soon became meager and bread had to be smuggled in, but
food parcels from abroad could arrrive until September,
1941, when the ghetto post office closed. After the United
States and Germany were at war, the Joint went under-
ground and managed to get substantial sums into Poland
through the services of the Swiss, Saly Mayer. By one
means or another these efforts continued even after May,
1943, when the ghettos were no more and the beneficiaries
were dispersed.

Russia, on the other hand, did not welcome the Joint at
all. The Soviets were willing to receive outside aid but resisted any suggestion of collaboration, insisting on ad-
ministering relief themselves. At the time, the stubbornness
of this ally was regarded as but temporary; the 1943 annual
meeting of the JDC even heard an optimistic rumor that the
Agro-Joint would shortly be reinstated. In fact, the Communists were unwilling to allow any foreigners to observe
conditions in the country and they had no intention of per-
mitting any activity that suggested the re-creation of Jewish
communal institutions.

France was within easier reach. The JDC was already
contributing to refugee organizations there before 1939. At
the German occupation in the spring of the following year,
it shifted its headquarters by way of Angers and Bordeaux
to Lisbon, but it also managed to keep an office going in
Marseilles. Until the Nazis absorbed the whole country, it
continued to help the work in the internment camps of the
Comité d'Assistance aux Réfugiés as well as the services of
OSE, ORT, HICEM and the Quakers, either smuggling
cash into Paris or allowing these groups to borrow against

the promise of ultimate Joint repayment. In 1943, such loans amounted to $140,000 a month. The Comité was able to sustain its work and even to contribute to the Resistance by such borrowings well after the Nazis were in full control.

The problems were similar although of shorter duration in Italy, Belgium and Holland, where the outbreak of war found a refugee as well as a native Jewish population exposed to the threat of German persecution. In 1940 and the early part of 1941 the Joint managed to do some good there; then the change in the military situation practically cut these places off from aid. The difficulties were greater still in Hungary, Rumania and Lithuania, where the numbers were larger and access harder. Nevertheless, Joint ingenuity got some assistance in and, in Hungary, managed miraculously to stave off the deportations for a while. Indeed, some packages even got across the very fences of the concentration camps, through the Red Cross and otherwise.

A very special problem existed in Asia. After September, 1939, the Soviet authorities moved between 350,000 and 400,000 Jews from their zone in Poland and from the Ukraine to Central Asia and Siberia. The situation of these migrants quickly became precarious, and after the German invasion of Russia, desperate. In the absence of resources, they succumbed to hunger and cold, and in 1942 only 150,000 were still alive, clustered in Kazakstan, Uzbekistan and Turkestan.

The Polish government in exile in London authorized the JDC to relieve its nationals, and for a time some aid under Russian control flowed through Murmansk. But the break in Russian-Polish relations interrupted that movement: the Soviets would allow the Joint to send parcels from Teheran only if they were addressed to specific individuals, were less than twelve pounds in weight and had the duty prepaid. Under these restrictions, Charles Passman managed to send off 250,000 packages at a cost of $5,000,000, of which $322,-

ooo went for postage and $1,700,000 for the Russian tariffs. The JDC did all the work and paid half the costs, the rest coming from other sources.

A smaller group of about 20,000 refugees from Central and Eastern Europe were stranded in Shanghai when the Japanese seized the city. Laura Margolis and Manuel Siegel, of the Joint staff, who were trapped with them, organized the settlement, got the poor to help the poorer, and negotiated loans against the promise of future payment. By these means they served the destitute thousands of meals a day. The Japanese tolerated the effort for months, but in the spring of 1943 interned the whole group. Yet in 1944, the enterprising Mr. Mayer got 237,000,000 Chinese dollars into the city to help keep them alive.

The pace of Joint work stepped up as the war approached its conclusion. When the Allies landed in Morocco and swept across North Africa, they exposed a whole new area of need. Refugee and native Jews alike were destitute; hundreds of them, huddled ragged and ill in bombed-out buildings while the temperature rose to 130 degrees, needed relief both to survive and to reconstruct communal institutions. Meanwhile, thousands of fugitives in Europe were maintained in hiding, and assistance extended into the very labor battalions through the channels developed by Saly Mayer out of Switzerland. In Croatia, Poland and elsewhere, supplies that could get in in no other way were dropped by parachute. When the JDC began to follow the advancing Allied armies into the liberated areas late in 1944, it could pick up old connections kept intact through the war.

Rescue operations, difficult as they were, at least had visible results. In 1939 the Joint was already all too familiar with the problem of finding homes for unwanted people. In that year, for instance, Morris Troper passed through endless agonies in the effort to find landing places for the 907 refugee passengers on the S.S. *St. Louis,* turned back from Cuba and headed for slavery if he failed. His successors were to repeat that experience many times.

In the first years of war, the JDC operated through two mechanisms. Under the clearance system, emigrants gave their currency to local Jewish welfare committees and the Joint, in return, paid for their passage in dollars. At an expense of $4,000,000, it thus saved 41,000 Germans, Austrians and Czechs. The Transmigration Bureau, set up in June, 1940, acted as a clearing house for Americans who financed the movement of refugee families, while the Joint paid the overhead. A year later the bureau staff of seventy was serving more than a hundred visitors a day in its office on West 14th Street in New York City. In less than two years it collected more than $5,000,000, part of which it used to help such families as it could trace. Although the balance was returned, the Joint also used its own funds to help those who lacked connections in the United States. A total of some 14,000 thus saved their lives by escape. When these methods became unusable after Pearl Harbor, the Joint devoted its own funds to the task of rescue. And of course, some of the relief sums it sent into occupied territory went for the purchase of false papers and assistance in flight. Its most sensational act of this sort came through Saly Mayer in the prolonged negotiations with the Nazis that liberated 1,673 Hungarian Jews and postponed the deportation of hundreds of thousands of others. Twenty thousand more Jews, in Budapest, were spared through the valiant efforts of Raoul Wallenberg, a Swedish businessman aided by JDC funds. Whatever dollars it put into such efforts had the approval of the United States Treasury, and after January, 1944, the cooperation of the War Refugee Board.

Palestine, the United States, Latin America, the Dutch

East and West Indies, the Congo and Australia were among the destinations. Switzerland offered shelter to some 25,000 Jews, and Sweden to a smaller number. But there was a tragic limit to the number of places, and even the fortunate holders of visas could not be sure of a safe arrival or of admittance. When Italy entered the war in June, 1940, the Mediterranean became unsafe for sea traffic. East Europeans thereafter struggled across Hungary and Rumania to the Black Sea; thence they crossed to Istanbul in coffin ships like the ill-fated *Struma*, which struck a mine with the loss of 800 lives. From Turkey they could try to slip into Palestine or else move eastward to Shanghai. Others went by rail across Siberia to Japan.

Marseilles and Casablanca were not long available as ports of embarkation. Lisbon therefore became the goal for Jews who wished to sail westward. In 1940, after the fall of France, it quickly acquired a population of 9,000 in transit, for whom Schwartz and his staff had to find shipping. In December the number had risen to 12,000, half of whom were still waiting five months later. In those two years, about 40,000 passed through the city. After Pearl Harbor, when it became difficult to secure passage, the Joint took to buying bulk space in vessels, paying up to $400,000 in advance, certain that there would be passengers enough for every berth. By one means or another, between 1939 and 1944 the JDC aided the emigration of 81,000 people who would otherwise have been added to the sum of Nazi victims.

When the Allied invasion of Italy reopened the Mediterranean, the tide of migration shifted toward Palestine. Hundreds made their way to the French and Italian seaports or to the Black Sea, hoping to find boats that would carry them away from Europe to their Promised Land.

The total who escaped to safety in the five years of war was pitifully small by comparison with the number doomed to remain. It was hardly a consolation that the remnant saved would be able to build new lives in new lands untouched by the bitter heritage of Europe's past.

While German-occupied territory took first priority in its thinking, the Joint could not afford to neglect the countries to which the refugees went. Apart from the desire to help the newcomers settle, there was an acute consciousness that the possibility of keeping the gates open depended upon the successful adjustment of the first arrivals.

The JDC had had almost thirty years of experience in Palestine. Its regional office in Jerusalem could continue its aid to cultural institutions and make grants for war relief, secure in the confidence that the Jewish Agency and the Yishuv would support immigration. In Turkey, Persia, Spain and Sweden, the numbers were relatively small and could be supported without excessive expense. The Jewish community of Switzerland had been generous to the fugitives in its midst, and when the Joint assumed the burden of their support, diverted its contributions to uses in Eastern Europe which a neutral could undertake and which a belligerent could not. But Joint help was essential in Portugal, which had few native Jews and where adequate provision for the transients was essential to keeping the channels of escape open.

Latin America was also important because it had space, because the refugees hoped to make permanent homes there and because its young Jewish communities were not themselves able to absorb the costs. In the ten years after 1933, some 113,000 newcomers had been added to a Jewish population of 463,000—an accretion of about 25 per cent. In Chile the number had more than doubled, in Ecuador more than tripled. The Joint spent some $700,000 a year in the region for medical and economic aid, and it established loan cooperatives in Argentina, Brazil and Ecuador. Indeed, in an effort to transplant the Agro-Joint techniques, the JDC helped set up a corporation to sponsor Jewish settlement in the Dominican Republic, in an experiment which only recruited a few hundred participants.

As the Allies secured a toehold on the continent of Europe and then painfully pushed the Germans back, they revealed an ominous perspective of the extent of the damage and of the need for reconstruction. The field workers who entered Italy, Poland and France could make a preliminary estimate toward the end of 1944. By the time of V-E Day, in May, 1945, the problems of the next decade were clear.

Outside the Soviet Union there were perhaps 1,500,000 survivors, some still in concentration camps, others stateless, adrift without homes or resources, many of them shattered in health. The whole society lay in ruins, in the midst of which the dispersed fragments of the Jewish communities seemed hopelessly lost. The 150,000 Jews who came back to Poland from the East gazed about them in amazement. "This was the end," one of them reflected. This empty desert—worse, this graveyard—"was the sum total of hundreds of generations of living and building, of religion, of Torah, of piety, of free thinking, of Zionism, of Bundism, of struggles and battles," of the aspirations of an entire people.

The only glimmer of hope lay in the possibility of assistance from America, from the only large body of Jews which had not suffered the scourge of German bestiality. To lend substance to that hope, the whole concept of overseas relief, as it had been known since 1914, required revision. Aid was no longer a form of charity but rather an obligation to rehabilitate in which costs did not count.

VII

AFTER THE

FINAL SOLUTION

1946-1952

BEFORE THE WAR was yet over the Jews of the United States had assumed the unprecedented responsibility of reconstructing the shattered lives of their co-religionists overseas. Between 1945 and 1952 they would spend $342,000,000 in the effort to do so.

In Western Europe a restored social order put success within their reach. In the East they failed. Behind the expanded boundaries of the Soviet Union almost three million Jews were sealed off from the rest of the world so that no help could reach them. Adverse conditions in the Communist satellites soon forced many of the remaining Jews there to depart; in 1952 Hitler's wish to empty Eastern Europe of its non-Aryans approached fulfillment.

That did not, however, end the work of the Joint. The

quest of the fugitives for a home touched off the chain of events that led to the independence of Israel; the war which brought that state into being created, in turn, new problems of relief in an uneasy Moslem world. In 1952 the Joint still had work to do.

The JDC by now was not only a permanent institution; it was a way of life to those active in it. Its structure reached deeply into every sector of Jewish life and permitted effective collaboration of volunteers and staff. Local meetings, regional conferences, documentary films and widely circulated publications established an involvement in its affairs; and a National Youth Advisory Council enlisted the aid of young people under thirty. The Joint, by 1952, had struck deep popular roots.

A National Council of 5,200 members (later almost double in size) met yearly and represented the constituency which exercised ultimate responsibility. It elected a Board of Directors of 210 (increased in 1947 to 350), the Executive Committee of which maintained regular liaison with operations through twelve subcommittees. The Executive Committee also designated an Administrative Committee, which met weekly and to which the departments reported. Continuity of both professional and lay leadership persisted. The only significant change came at Hyman's retirement in 1947, when Leavitt took his place and Louis H. Sobel became secretary. The staff in New York and overseas had expanded to about 2,500, 10 per cent of them Americans. For short periods even larger numbers were on the payroll.

The United Jewish Appeal now was also a fixture, capable of making radically increased demands for funds. Henry Montor and Isidor Coons demonstrated this in 1946, when they dramatically raised the sights of the campaign above $100,000,000 for the first time. That effort was to be quickly surpassed. The 1947 goal of $170,000,000 seemed startling only until the $250,000,000 target of 1948 was announced. Requirements eased somewhat thereafter, but still came to $151,500,000 in 1952. Relationships between the UJA and the Joint were close—so intimate indeed that Warburg and Schwartz in 1951 took over the direction of the United Jewish Appeal.

With the aid of the UJA, the Joint's income rose from slightly more than $20,000,000 in 1945 to $72,000,000 in 1948, and while it declined thereafter, still stood at $21,000,-000 in 1952. Since the organization also was ready to borrow when necessary, it could expand its activities rapidly. Expenditures climbed from about $25,000,000 in 1945 to a height of $69,000,000 in 1947 and were still close to $19,000,000 in 1952. Supplementary contributions came from Canada, South Africa, England, Argentina, Uruguay and Brazil, and special drives, like SOS (Supplies for Overseas Survivors), produced 14,000,000 pounds of food; 11,000,000 pounds of clothing; 75,000 layettes; 1,000,000 capsules of drugs; and 180,000 toys and other donations in kind between January, 1946 and April, 1949.

The gratifying response owed much to the education of American Jews in their obligations. The shock of learning that the wartime rumors had been all too true, and the exposure to the realities of the camps, stimulated generosity. The emergence of the State of Israel generated a sense of pride and a determination to carry the work of reconstruction forward. The rising status of the Jews in the United States, the heightened sense of personal identification with the group and the general prosperity of the nation also contributed to the willingness and the ability to give. These conditions generated the resources that the Joint would expend on relief and reconstruction, on migration and on resettlement in Israel and elsewhere.

Relief called for more than money. It took logistic skill to procure and ship 226,767,750 pounds of supplies from the United States, in addition to great quantities of goods from South Africa, Canada and Latin America. It took imagination to conceive that the helpless wrecks in the concentration camps could become self-supporting men. And it took human sympathy to arouse the desire to rebuild among those who had seen all the work of their lives reduced to rubble.

The United Nations Relief and Rehabilitation Administration, established in 1943, was a valuable ally. It had official status, considerable funds of its own, and access to supplies; and it was led by Governor Herbert H. Lehman, who retained close connections with the Joint. The International Refugee Organization, which supplanted UNRRA at the end of June, 1947, lacked the same resources; thereafter the Joint had to bear a greater share of the burden.

When the war ended, relief operations were already in process for the 1,500,000 Jews still alive in Europe. The JDC was then supporting soup kitchens in France and rounding up the 8,000 children hidden during the occupation. In Belgium 20,000 Jews came out of concealment and called for assistance; in North Africa, 1,000 refugees awaited rescue; in Rumania and Hungary hundreds of thousands were dependent; and in Shanghai, Manuel Siegel still was struggling to keep alive more than 15,000 men and women under his charge. While meeting these emergency demands, it was also necessary to think of cultural aid and of the reunion of families through the Central Location

Index, which the JDC sponsored along with other international agencies.

When the Joint first entered upon these activities it could deal only with crises. It was giving succor of some sort to 750,000 persons in 1946, to fully a million a year later. The important thing then was to hunt out scarce supplies in a shortage-bound world, to get an equitable share of Army surplus property, to arrange transportation, and to keep track of the stray survivors in every part of the world.

High priority went to the displaced persons, the hundreds of thousands who had been deported by the Germans or had fled from the advancing Reds, and who now, far from home, were housed in camps until they could be repatriated. First the Army and then UNRRA were responsible for feeding these people. But the Joint also had a function. It insisted that the Jews be separated in establishments of their own rather than mingled by nationality with people who might be hostile, and it supplemented the meager official rations in an effort to compensate for the deprivations of the past. It knew that more than bread was required; rescue also involved equipping the distressed to go out into the world as self-supporting individuals. The camps smacked of the past; they undermined personal responsibility and family solidarity; and they extended the sense of dependence. The sooner they were closed the better.

Yet these places were not readily emptied; the 100,000 Jews who lived there at V-E Day had become 250,000 in 1947 as their numbers were swollen by fugitives from the East, and as a high birth rate offset departures. By then UNRRA was dissolved and the JDC employed 2,000 personnel, including hundreds of doctors, to care for these people to whom it supplied an average of 224,000 rations daily. In Germany alone it maintained 67 schools, 47 kindergartens and 75 talmud torahs, and it printed newspapers, magazines and books in many languages, for it counted education as important as food. In cooperation with the Central Committee of Liberated Jews, representing the displaced persons, it launched an employment and vocational training program and furnished $800,000 worth of machinery and materials for work projects, all to the end of teaching the DP's to sustain themselves.

In the first half of 1948 morale declined. Patience ran thin as long as people remained uncertain where they would go, and the staff faced serious problems of administration. Then Israeli independence and, to a much lesser extent, the American Displaced Persons Act opened the channels of migration. In subsequent years, the camp population declined as resettlement opportunities became available. In 1949 fewer than 50,000 remained; by the end of 1952 only 15,500 hard-core cases were left.

In the immediate postwar years the need for relief was general throughout Europe and North Africa. The demand for medical aid was not confined to the camps. In 1946, 20 per cent of the Joint budget went to health; the Merano sanitarium, opened that year, began the long fight against tuberculosis; and a dental-care program was instituted. Two years later the JDC was treating 106,000 patients in 529 hospitals and other institutions. To multiply the effect of its efforts it also undertook to educate nurses and to retrain local doctors and dentists. It continued to work for improved health, in collaboration with OSE and TOZ, down to the end of the period.

The old concerns with education and cultural development and with vocational training also persisted. In 1947, the Joint contributed to the support of 140,000 children in

382 centers and elsewhere, and it extended some form of educational aid to 110,000 persons in 1948. It supported hundreds of synagogues, schools and community institutions, and it subsidized scholars to resume their studies. By 1950 it had published 1,000,000 copies of 189 books in Persian, Hebrew, Yiddish, French, German, Italian, Rumanian, Polish, Hungarian, Czech and English; and for some years it had supported a Yiddish theater in Munich. The hope that the Jews of each locality would be able to support these activities themselves was not immediately realized. In 1950 the JDC still maintained 285 schools in some twenty different countries.

It had also tried immediately to equip with skills those capable of working. In 1948 it was helping 78,520 do so. But for the long run it preferred to transfer that responsibility to ORT, which had great experience in the field. An agreement, negotiated in 1947 and annually renewed, provided that organization with subventions of between $1,000,000 and $2,000,000 a year to permit it to do the job.

After the peak of the emergency, the effectiveness of the Joint program varied greatly from country to country. In the West, in 1952, restored Jewish communities thrived and grew in strength and size. In the East, the Nazi final solution was becoming a reality: the Jews were disappearing.

In France, Belgium, Holland and Italy, the establishment of stable democratic governments, Marshall Plan help and economic recovery created a favorable environment which attracted Jews out of the camps and from the East. In 1947 between 1,500 and 2,000 were entering France each month; about 1,300 were crossing the Italian frontiers. Many of these people were in transit to Israel, but some stayed. As a result, the Jewish population of these countries increased.

The number in France rose from 200,000 in 1946 to 300,000 in 1952, in Belgium from 30,000 to 45,000. Joint assistance, loan cooperatives, an employment service and vocational aid made these people self-supporting, so that the number of recipients of aid in the same period in France sank from 65,450 to 15,000. Meanwhile local institutions recovered their vitality; the Fonds Social Juif Unifié, with JDC guidance, organized philanthropy after the American pattern, and the Paul Baerwald School of Social Work, near Paris, began to train professionals in the field.

Down to 1948 the situation was somewhat similar in North Africa, which had strong connections with France. The Vichy regime had raised the disturbing question of the citizenship of the Jews in Algeria, Morocco and Tunisia. But its laws were reversed after its downfall, and for a few years after the peace, the region required little external assistance. In the areas under Western control there was cause for optimism about the effectiveness of JDC aid.

Eastern Europe, by contrast, seemed beyond the possibility of recovery. Repeated efforts to save the remnants of once powerful communities met invariable frustration. Immediately after the war the Joint sent some $1,500,000 worth of medicine into the Soviet Union; but attempts thereafter to re-establish contact with the 3,000,000 Jews of that country came to nothing. Meanwhile Poland, Hungary, Rumania, Bulgaria and Czechoslovakia, the scenes of bitter memories, fell into the hands of totalitarian regimes uncongenial to free men; there, the nationalization of enterprise and rigid political controls made life difficult for such Jews as had survived or considered returning. Only in Greece were a few of them able to establish themselves successfully.

Those who during the war had hidden in the forests or

had lost themselves in the cities, emerged when the Germans left; those who had fled or had been deported now came back. They found themselves in a wilderness: Vilna, Kovno, Breslau, Warsaw, Pressburg, the great names of their culture, were wiped out. The handful of survivors, their families dispersed or dead, tried to pick up the loose ends of their lives, but without ever knowing which among their neighbors had shared the guilt of the Nazis, which had been only silent onlookers. The more energetic thought of leaving. The question was, Where?

As it was, the numbers were sadly reduced—little more than 850,000 in all of Eastern Europe outside the Soviet Union. Because of the shifting national boundaries and the uncertain conditions of the time, a precise count was impossible; the total fluctuated from year to year, almost from month to month, as some individuals drifted back to their homes while others gave up and emigrated.

Just after the peace, there seem to have been 380,000 Jews in Rumania, 150,000 in Hungary, 220,000 in Poland, 45,000 in Bulgaria, 42,000 in Czechoslovakia and 15,000 in Yugoslavia, many of them repatriates, most of them dependent. People in the prime of life were either dead or had departed; the very young and the very old remained. There were many more women than men.

The tasks of the Joint were clear and imperative. It set up canteens for the hungry, schools and homes for the children, hospitals for the ill. As in the past, there was also an effort to reorganize communal institutions and to develop economic independence. By the end of 1947 the Central Committee of Polish Jews and the two hundred producers' cooperatives in that country seemed evidence of a "remarkable comeback." In Hungary, loan societies and workshops, and in Czechoslovakia, Bulgaria and Rumania, producers' cooperatives and vocational training projects gave grounds for similar optimism.

But almost from the start there were indications that developments in the East would differ from those in the West. On July 4, 1946, a mob in the Polish town of Kielce broke out in a pogrom that gave a bitter foretaste of the nature of the welcome the Jews would receive. Shortly after the coup in Czechoslovakia, the other Communist regimes became more repressive and there were open inclinations toward anti-Semitic measures, both in the Soviet Union and in the satellites. Hungary arrested the JDC director, Israel Jacobson, on a charge of espionage. In December, 1949, Poland expelled the Joint and confiscated all its establishments; a month later, Czechoslovakia did the same; and Hungary would only permit operations through the local community. Meanwhile a famine in Rumania in 1947 had added to the general distress.

The signs were clear. Once more the Jews began to leave, although they sometimes had to do so illegally, for even where they were not wanted there were laws against emigration. By 1952 fewer than 50,000 remained in Poland, fewer than 20,000 in Czechoslovakia and fewer than 7,000 in Bulgaria. In the whole region there were less than half of the 850,000 of 1945.

Dismal conditions everywhere and the failure of reconstruction in Eastern Europe emphasized the importance of migration. Even before the war was over, small groups of Jews were on the move with Joint help. After 1947 the JDC devoted an increasing share of its budget, directly or indirectly, to aid in getting them away. It could not afford to hesitate; in many cases it was now or never, departure or doom. In all, it was to assist 623,000 persons from every part of Europe, Asia and North Africa in leaving their native places for new homes.

Visas and entry permits remained precious. Nothing that

had happened since 1933—not even the revelation of the horrors of the camps—had eased the restrictive laws in the United States. The McCarran-Walter Act of 1952 kept the same limitations and reflected the same prejudices as the law of 1924. The Displaced Persons Act of 1948 opened the gates to some 250,000 victims of the European disaster but contained features that held down the number of Jews eligible to enter. It was only with difficulty that a cutoff provision was modified which excluded from the benefits of the law displaced persons who had entered the camps after 1945. In any case, bureaucratic delays in the consular service were often time- and energy-consuming. Australia and Canada were somewhat more liberal than they had been before 1939, for they had now come to value European manpower, whether it was Anglo-Saxon or not. Some Latin American countries were also willing to absorb moderate numbers.

The Joint took advantage of all these opportunities. Between the end of the war and 1952, it aided about 100,000 Jews to these destinations, about two thirds of them to the United States. Gratifying as that migration was, it left unsolved the problem of the larger contingents who wished to leave and for whom these countries did not wish to make space.

There remained Palestine. Even during the war some Jews had been able to take refuge there if they fell within or could evade the British limitations. After the peace many more bent their steps in that direction, particularly those who were determined never again to be a minority, never again to trust Christian or Islamic society. Escape groups formed to make their way to Palestine, legally or illegally, and various Zionist groups encouraged them to do so.

In accordance with its general nonpolitical stance, the Joint had refused to take sides in the controversy over the mandate's future; its membership encompassed all shades of Zionist and non-Zionist opinion and it aided those who needed help wherever they were. In the Europe of 1945, it insisted that the choice should be that of the victims: to remain where the fortunes of war had left them, or to go back to their native lands, or to migrate where they wished when the law permitted it. But increasingly it became clear that the Jews were not welcome in Eastern Europe and that the only place to which they could go in substantial numbers was Palestine.

As a practical matter, therefore, the Joint found itself involved in furthering the migration to Palestine. From every part of Central and Eastern Europe groups of determined Jews set forth in 1946—openly when the governments permitted them to depart, otherwise surreptitiously. They made their way first to occupied Germany, Austria or Italy and then with the aid of Zionist escape organizations to the seaports—Marseilles, Spezia, Bari and Constantsa—where they hoped that Mossad, the Palestinian Committee for Illegal Immigration, would find them the shipping across the Mediterranean or the Black Sea. En route, the Joint was available to help; it permitted some of its funds to be siphoned into all of these activities.

It would not, however, itself break the law, for that would endanger its operations everywhere, and the mandatory power still held to the restrictive policy of the White Paper of 1939. Earl Harrison, representative of the Intergovernmental Committee on Refugees in 1945, had asked for a relaxation of that policy in order to permit the admission to Palestine of 100,000 newcomers. He had been refused, and the same fate befell the similar suggestion of the Anglo-American commission of inquiry in April, 1946. The British could not see their way clear to meet demands that might alienate the Arabs and undermine their position in the Near

East. The eager immigrants were turned back from their goal, many to be cooped up in internment camps on Cyprus, which held as many as 34,000 in 1947. The Joint supplied these people with food, clothing, medicine and vocational training. But it could not resolve the major problem of their future. A special concession by the British in 1947 permitted the entry of 6,000 children. That was all.

Pressure from those who sought admission and London's intransigence brought the situation in the Holy Land to a crisis. The Jews of the Yishuv would not stand idly by while their brethren were turned away; yet the Arabs feared each new arrival. Soon the two groups exploded into open warfare. The UN attempted vainly to mediate and Britain, unable to please either side, withdrew. In the power vacuum that followed in 1948, the State of Israel proclaimed its independence; and a brief war with its Arab neighbors finally led to an uneasy armistice. With the gates then open to all who would enter, the flow of migrants mounted steadily.

Israeli independence settled the Zionist issue. The question of whether Jews should or should not form a separate political entity became irrelevant; the state actually existed. In the perspective of the Joint that made all the difference in the world. It could now aid the Jews of that country as it did those of any other without thereby taking a political position, and it could now openly support migration there.

It was a relief to be able to close cases that had been pending for years. The last inmates left the camps of Cyprus in February, 1949. Those worrisome Shanghai refugees also could now find homes; 14,000 of those people had escaped to Israel and other countries by the time the Chinese Communists took control of that city. A Near Eastern example was even more dramatic. Back in 1943, some 2,000 Yemenite refugees had drifted into the British protectorate of Aden, where they barely survived a typhoid epidemic. With Joint funds Dr. Olga Feinberg organized a camp which attracted a steadily growing population. There they still languished five years later. The 50,000 hopeless Yemenites in Aden and in their native land were the victims of riots in December, 1947; but seven months after independence almost all of them were on the way to Israel in planes chartered from Alaska Airlines. That the aircraft designed to carry 56 passengers had to take on 125 to 145 caused no great difficulty; life in Aden had reduced the weight of the average adult male to eighty pounds. Operation Magic Carpet brought out 5,000 at once and the rest soon after at a cost to the Joint of $4,000,000.

Parodoxically, Israeli independence increased the number of potential immigrants. A wave of nationalistic resentment passed through the Arab world in the course of the war of 1948. Riots in Aden, Morocco and Tripoli and hostile governmental attitudes in Iraq, Syria and Egypt persuaded some Jews in those countries that their future was far from secure. Fully 32,000 of the 35,000 in Libya promptly left. Operation Ezra in 1950 brought thousands of Kurdish and Iraqi Jews to Lydda from Baghdad by way of Nicosia at a cost to the Joint of $2,500,000. They joined the greater tide that flowed toward Israel from Europe. In the year after independence nearly 240,000 from all sources reached their Promised Land, 85 per cent of them with help from the JDC. By the end of 1952 the total had gone above 700,000.

There was some anomaly, after independence, to Joint operations in a sovereign Jewish state which had its own channels for appeal to the United States. The Zionist organizations, linked to the government through the Jewish Agency, now demanded exclusive control over aid connected with immigration. Indeed, the more extreme and less responsible elements sought to turn all overseas relief into an instrument for recruiting settlers for Israel, and looked askance at the Joint program which made it possible for Jews to remain in Europe and Africa who might otherwise have migrated to Israel.

More powerful influences worked toward an accommodation, however. The government of the State and the United Jewish Appeal were equally apprehensive about the consequences of an open quarrel, and there was, in fact, work enough for all. By 1952 there was a well-understood division of efforts: the Jewish Agency controlled the actual process of immigration, reception and settlement, while the Joint continued its own operations outside Israel and, inside the country, undertook certain defined relief and cultural activities.

The Malben agreement between Israel and the Joint in 1949 illustrated the adjustment. The government, having opened the gates of the country to all Jews, was troubled by the high proportion of dependents among the newcomers. The needs of the aged and handicapped could not be neglected, and yet, the nation's energies were focused on the tasks of construction. It was therefore eager to have the JDC take over the burden. The Joint, for its part, was then supporting thousands of aged and handicapped "hard core" cases in Europe, who would not be accepted elsewhere. It was eager to provide them with a permanent place of settlement and rehabilitation.

According to the agreement, the two parties undertook to provide the financing for a new agency, Malben, which would assume the charge of people already in Israel, house them all in proper institutions and do what could be done to rehabilitate them through medical care, retraining and workshops. Some $15,000,000 were initially allocated for the task. The human need in this case overrode all other considerations. In 1950, after one year of joint operations, the JDC took over the financing and administration of Malben with the agreement that the agency's clientele would be the eligible, needy immigrants who came to Israel after the State was established.

From 1948 onward, North Africa and the Moslem world in general demanded increasing attention. The Joint had earlier made some small grants to the ancient Jewish communities in those regions and after the Nazi invasions had aided the refugees in North Africa. But the disturbances caused by the war for Israeli independence revealed the fundamental problems of life there. Cooped up in ghettos in a society that had resisted change for centuries, the Jews existed precariously. Even the 500,000 in Tunisia, Algeria and Morocco, where French rule then offered some protection, suffered from poverty, overcrowding, disease and high mortality rates. Those in immediate danger, as in Iraq and Egypt, had to be assisted to migrate. In North Africa and Iran, where a peaceful adjustment was at least possible, those who wished to stay needed aid in raising their standard of existence.

In the next three years the Joint program there expanded rapidly. With ORT it provided vocational training for almost 4,000. Through the schools of the Alliance Israélite Universelle it aided the education of 60,000. In cooperation with OSE it treated more than 40,000 patients a month in 75 medical institutions. And in addition, it furnished substantial amounts of direct relief, especially to children.

After 1950 the Joint cut back its operations. In 1951 its expenditures fell to about $20,000,000, in 1952 to about

$19,000,000. Eastern Europe, the DP's, migration—its most important concerns in the past—had all shrunk in importance. The staff both in New York and abroad was reduced to some 200, and promotional activity was curtailed in anticipation of a more stable future. The JDC still contributed to the support of some 200,000 individuals around the world and there was no thought now, as there had been in a more innocent postwar period, of going out of existence. But the emergency was over.

VIII

A CONTINUING TASK

1952-1964

A WORLD THAT CONTINUED to change continued also to make work for the Joint. The troubles of the Jewish survivors in Eastern Europe were far from over; having lived through the perils of Fascism, they now faced those of Communism. Their more fortunate co-religionists in the West and in Israel prospered, but they still required American aid and guidance. And the Moslem world, now beginning to change rapidly, generated ugly problems that persisted into the 1960's. Nowhere had the need for JDC services ended. Overseas relief remained a continuing task of the Jews of the United States.

Behind the Iron Curtain, the Communist regimes struggled fitfully to maintain political control and to stimulate economic growth. Although often obscured by censorship, the popular mood fluctuated from sullen apathy to momentary resistance, and then to resignation. Hostility to Russian domination reached its peak in Hungary during the summer of 1956 but subsided after the failure of the abortive revolt. Ultimately, Stalinist repressiveness throughout the region gave way to the thaw of the period of coexistence. But meanwhile, the position of the Jews had deteriorated further from its low point in 1952. The nationalization of trade and industry had already destroyed their economic role. Now the "doctors' plot" in Russia, the Slansky trial in Czechoslovakia, accusations that the Joint engaged in espionage, and the linkage of Jews with imperialism—all lent respectability to the residual anti-Semitism of the masses. In addition, the Soviet Union, inspired by the desire to court Arab friendship, occasionally linked Zionism with imperialism and thus further stirred up distrust of the Jews.

In all of Eastern Europe only the few thousand Jews in Tito's Yugoslavia could feel at all secure. The 3,000,000 in Russia were totally out of reach of foreign organizations; hemmed in by a government determined to disregard their identity, they winced frequently at accusations of cosmopolitanism. The 150,000 who remained in Hungary lost their most important source of assistance in January, 1953, when the Joint was compelled to terminate operations there. In increasing numbers they sought to leave; some 18,000 fled in the aftermath of the revolution of 1956 alone. By the end of 1963 fewer than 75,000 remained.

Poland received a sudden addition to its Jewish population in 1957 when the Soviet Union repatriated 20,000 who had been lost in the East for more than a decade. In the aftermath of that unexpected development, late that year, the government invited the JDC to resume work in the country. The Joint supplied food, aid to children, medical assistance and construction loans through an indigenous central committee with branches in fourteen cities. Within two years it was serving some 40,000 beneficiaries. Many of these people nevertheless grasped eagerly at any opportunity to depart, and the JDC helped them on their way. At the end of 1963 there remained perhaps 260,000 in all of Eastern Europe—the region whose needs had first called the Joint into being.

In Austria and Germany the story was somewhat happier. The last of the camps—at Föhrenwald near Munich—closed down in 1957 when the remaining DP's, who clung intransigently to their DP status, finally left. Some Jews stayed permanently in this area, trying to forget the past and to rebuild anew. Austria indeed was able to receive, at least temporarily, 18,000 of the refugees who had fled from Budapest in 1956. In Germany those who could stifle memories were relatively well off. Although the Jewish population increased from 32,000 to 40,000, after 1952 the extent of dependence upon the Joint diminished and what need remained was largely for cultural services. In 1964, this old center of Jewish life seemed unlikely to produce new problems. But it also seemed no more likely than the East to become a nucleus for future growth or creativity.

The situation was far different in the countries of Western Europe, where astounding economic recovery in the 1950's established the basis both for a growing Jewish population and for a healthy communal life. In France, Italy, Belgium and the Netherlands the number of native and immigrant Jews rose from 419,000 in 1952 to 600,000 in 1962, most of the increase having come in the first-named nation. Elsewhere in non-Communist Europe—in Scandinavia, Greece and the Iberian Peninsula—the size and the

situation of the Jewish group remained stable. In most of
these places efforts could now deal with normal problems.
The Fonds Social of Paris grew stronger, for instance; and
the Oeuvre de Protection des Enfants Juifs, originally established to help French children, was able to contribute to
the support of those in less fortunate areas.

JDC activities in Western Europe and in Latin America
and Australia—the other parts of the world that remained
relatively peaceful—followed well-tested patterns. The
indigenous community was expected to meet its own philanthropic obligations as soon as possible; the Joint sustained
incoming refugees and furnished supplementary aid for exceptional needs.

Recognizing that the war had left long-range problems
of dependency and reconstruction, for example, it supplied
some medical assistance and helped erect old-age homes,
schools and communal structures. There seemed a special
significance in the fact that contributions from American
Jews should rebuild the ancient synagogue of Venice, and
after almost five hundred years, bring the traditional forms
of worship back to Madrid. Each project completed, in
Stockholm or Rome or Antwerp, was evidence of the
permanence of the work of reconstruction.

Joint-assisted loan institutions meanwhile provided thousands with the means of attaining economic independence,
in Paris as in Montevideo, in Athens as in Melbourne. In
1958, 38 such organizations operated in 19 countries. The
JDC also continued its relationship with ORT, which it
subsidized to the extent of about $1,500,000 a year for voca-
tional training. Furthermore, from 1950 onward it distributed throughout the world millions of pounds of surplus
commodities donated by the United States Department of
Agriculture under the Food for Peace program.

The fact that the number of recipients of aid in Western

Europe and Latin America actually rose from about 22,500 in 1952 to about 76,000 in 1962 was a sign of prosperity, for most of the increase was due to renewed migration. The volume varied from year to year according to conditions in Eastern Europe and in the Moslem world. It reached one high point between the end of 1956 and 1958 after the events in Hungary and Suez, then it subsided in 1959 and 1960, but it rose again in 1961 and 1962. Each movement demanded a quick response by the Joint to assist its victims; Brazil, for instance, could not have received the 3,300 newcomers it did, in the first nine months of 1957, without such help.

The Joint was no longer directly involved in migration to Israel. But its role in the Jewish state remained substantial. On the average it allocated about 40 per cent of its budget to activities there.

Israel passed through a perilous decade after independence. Its Arab neighbors, still unreconciled to its existence, refused to make peace and threatened to drive its people into the sea. The inescapable costs of defending a long border thus threatened, compelled the diversion of precious funds to military needs and forced the population to live under garrison conditions. Repeated incursions by Fedayin guerrilla bands, frequent border clashes and annoying economic reprisals persuaded the Israelis to join the French and the British in the Suez attack. Although the three invaders withdrew their forces in response to a UN vote, the outcome of the incident was a greater degree of stability than had existed before. Immigration resumed, the population rose from 1,450,000 in 1952 to 2,155,500 in 1963, and economic development proceeded steadily.

Most educational and cultural needs were no longer a

responsibility of the Joint. However, it continued its traditional program of aid to *yeshivoth*, the number of which
reached 105 in 1963 with over 12,000 students. The Joint's
activities in Israel took a familiar form and they reached a
widening circle of beneficiaries; the number helped rose
dramatically from 30,000 in 1952 to 86,430 in 1963. Cash
and food relief that year still went to 35,985 dependent
persons. Sixteen JDC-supported homes sheltered 4,000 aged.
The Malben program continued, marked by the opening
of a 500-bed hospital for tuberculars in 1953, a year
in which the budget of the organization amounted to
$12,000,000. Rising costs in this country, however, were
made tolerable by the consciousness that they generated
hope for the possibility of permanent improvement.

Therein the experience in Israel differed from that in
the Moslem lands. By 1952, increasing involvement with
the fate of the Jews in North Africa and the Near East
had only begun to produce an awareness of the dimensions
of their problems. Beyond the surface evidence of Arab
hostility, dramatic as that was, lay a deeper cause for concern. The traditional Jewish communities were socially,
culturally and economically incapable of adjusting unaided
to the changing conditions of their times.

Their situation was remarkably analogous to that of the
Eastern Europeans forty years earlier. Here too they were
entirely separate. In many places the Jews actually lived in
the walled-off *mellah*, or ghetto; elsewhere they stood apart
from their Islamic neighbors not only in religion but also in
dress, habits, occupations and language, and sometimes even
in a distinct legal status. The basis for mutual understanding
was therefore distressingly thin.

The growth of Arab nationalism complicated the problem. To the extent that Jews modernized their behavior and left the ghetto, they moved toward European models and identified themselves with the English, the French and the Israelis rather than with the culture about them, for the Moslem *medinah* was as backward as their own *mellah*. As a result, they were establishing a link with the imperialist Western forces, which all Arab nationalists regarded as their antagonists. Israel's presence was an irritating reminder of that connection, and each liberation movement along the southern rim of the Mediterranean and in the Near East contained elements of danger to the Jews.

Above all, the economic situation was precarious. A large proportion of the Jews were poor, trapped in the stagnant occupations of petty trade and artisanry, and weakened by miserable living conditions and endemic disease. In North Africa, trachoma—a reliable index of poverty and filth— afflicted 60 per cent. Yet efforts to improve the productive system as a whole tended to weaken rather than help the Jews, because most measures for the modernization of agriculture and industry restricted the traditional role of these people.

The JDC program was already in operation here in 1952. Thereafter, between 15 and 20 per cent of the budget went to the needs of this area. Loan cooperatives in which ICA also participated, vocational training through ORT and schools operated by the Alliance aimed to further economic adjustment. Grants of clothing and food tided the needy over, and special aid came at the time of such disasters as the Agadir earthquake. Meanwhile an extensive medical effort with OSE began to cope with the immense deficiencies in health that sapped the vitality of the population. Even the needs of the obscure B'nei Israel in India were now discovered. Characteristically, after having trained a hundred social workers in Paris, the Baerwald School closed its doors and sent its staff off to the more complex problems of North Africa. (The name would later be applied to a new school in the Hebrew University in Jerusalem that introduced modern social-work concepts to Israel.)

Nevertheless, the number of recipients of help in the Moslem areas increased by less than 10 per cent between 1952 and 1962—from 91,000 to 98,200—and in 1963 declined to 83,980. The reason was not hard to find. The Jewish population of these countries in the same years shrank from 578,000 to 214,000, almost entirely as a result of emigration. The movement outward had continued since the Arab war with Israel, and the events of the 1950's stimulated it. Repressive measures in the aftermath of the Suez crisis drove out 25,000 Jewish residents of Egypt in 1957 alone. The removal of French authority—first in Tunisia, then in Morocco and finally in Algeria—also caused profound uneasiness and increased the number of departures. And each of these events had repercussions far beyond the boundaries of the country in which it occurred. The Jews in every Islamic land had reason to worry about their future; and many decided that safety lay only in migration. In 1961 some 80,000 refugees were in motion, about half of them to Israel, 30,000 to France. In the next years the total was considerably larger.

The Jewish Agency was primarily responsible for the movement into Israel, but the Joint bore some of the costs of relief to the socially handicapped persons there. And it had to aid directly the substantial numbers who chose to go to France or other countries. Such charges formed an important part of its expenditures in the whole period, and the problem still remained in 1964. The task that the Joint Distribution Committee had assumed in Poland and Russia in 1914 still occupied it in Morocco and Iran a half century later.

. . .

Experience and continuity of personnel lent stability to the organization. Warburg remained chairman, and many members of the National Council, the Board of Directors and the lay committees had years of service behind them. Leavitt was still the head of the operating staff, combining the roles of executive vice-chairman and secretary. Schwartz, however, did not return from his leave to the UJA. His place as director-general went first to Moses W. Beckelman and then to Charles H. Jordan. For many years, there have been two able assistant directors-general, Herbert Katzki and Samuel Haber. Jordan, who had had a long career of active service in the field, was prepared to adapt JDC work in response to the new conditions of the 1950's and 1960's. He, for instance, helped organize the Standing Conference of Jewish Communal Service, comprising central Jewish agencies of fourteen countries, meeting regularly to discuss common problems and to coordinate financial efforts. Some of the communities which had only recently been receiving aid themselves, now began to help the less fortunate.

Much of the excitement of fund raising in earlier years was gone, along with much of the uncertainty. The habit of giving was well established; American Jews were prosperous and aware of their continuing obligations; and the United Jewish Appeal operated with the efficiency of a well-oiled apparatus. Divisive conflicts were also less important than formerly. Occasional attacks upon the Joint's non-political attitude, as in 1953, did little damage; and as the old distinction between Zionist and non-Zionist lost relevance, mutual understanding and collaboration became characteristic.

The Conference on Jewish Material Claims against Germany was evidence of the capacity of various sectors of world Jewry to work together. Its moving spirit was Nahum Goldmann, and it elicited the collaboration of 23 organizations, among them the Joint. The purpose of the conference was to administer the funds paid by the German government under an agreement of September, 1952, as a token compensation for the damages done the Jews under the Nazi regime. About $10,000,000 a year became available from this source, 70 per cent of which was allocated to the Joint for its labors of relief and rehabilitation.

As a result, the budget remained quite stable and enabled the JDC, in all parts of the world, to assist a roster of beneficiaries that rose from 178,000 in 1952 to 262,000 in 1963. Income, after having fallen to a postwar low of $21,000,000 in 1952, recovered and fluctuated between $25,000,000 and $29,000,000 from 1954 onward. Expenditures fell within the same range. While these figures were below the astronomical heights of 1948, they were substantially higher than those of any year before the end of the Second World War. They reflected the continuing conviction of the Jews of the United States that the Joint still had a job to do.

In its half-century history the American Jewish Joint Distribution Committee meant many things to many men.

To the recipients of its aid it often meant the difference between life and death. Into the Galician *shtetl* devastated by Cossack invaders, and into the stifling *mellah* pillaged by the unruly mob, it brought not only bread but also the promise of future reconstruction on a basis sounder than in the past.

To its contributors it meant an opportunity to express their Jewish identity through humanitarianism. To them, the adjustment to America had often demanded the abandonment or modification of ancient traditions and rituals in return for progress and had left even the most successful with a sense of loss. Through their gifts to the less fortunate elsewhere, the Jews of the United States reached out to their own past by affirming the connection with those who still suffered the penalties of a common heritage.

To its staff the Joint meant a life of service. Many of these workers were but a generation removed from the East European origins of those they helped. Increasingly, the field workers and administrators were professionals, trained to careers of social aid, and they regarded themselves as front-line fighters in a war against human deterioration. Some indeed lost their lives in the struggle. All were called upon to exercise diplomacy in relations with foreigners; financial skill in the management of other peoples' money; and tact in preserving the dignity of the people they aided.

To all—staff, donors and beneficiaries—the JDC stood for the willingness to sacrifice. The whole enterprise was voluntary and therefore depended upon the ability of men to feel for one another, not only to understand the problems of the less fortunate but to wish to share them. It was this sense of involvement that most impressed outsiders who observed the operations of the Joint.

Yet there was also a larger meaning to the experience of the JDC, one which emerged in the actions of its founders and which has persisted through the fifty years of its history. The generation of Schiff and Marshall was in transition, not only in the sense that its members were immigrants or the children of immigrants, but also in the extent to which they were moving from old to new social and cultural conceptions. Valuing their Judaism, which they wished to make relevant to their New World, they seized upon the idea of *zedakah*, which they interpreted as social justice and which they made central to their faith. The Joint was one of the ways in which they tried to put into practice their belief in the Fatherhood of God and the Brotherhood of man.

That was why they so long regarded the organization they formed as temporary and so eagerly anticipated its dissolution: the inhumanity that caused the call for its assistance surely could not long endure. They looked forward to the not distant moment when the Jews would be ready for the world and the world ready for the Jews. The Joint's task was to help the East European Jews survive the trial of war and to emerge from their ghettos as free and equal citizens of a modern society.

This was a noble dream, but one made illusory by the nationalism and the economic disorder of the 1920's and 1930's. In the end, East European Jewry was totally destroyed, and the Joint faced in the 1960's an ominously similar problem in the Moslem countries. The world was not yet ready for the Jews.

The healthy growing communities of Western Europe and Israel are evidence of the effectiveness of the Joint's efforts in a beneficent climate. But success or failure is not the proper criterion by which to judge the worth of its activities. In Poland and in Morocco, as much as in happier lands, it comforted the distressed and lifted up the poor. It kept the faith in social justice and in the brotherhood of man in a world that urgently needed reminders of those values. That is its enduring meaning.